Making
TERRIFIC
SCRAPBOOK PAGES

We love scrapbooking! In 1996, Hot Off The Press was the very first company to develop papers exclusively for scrapbookers. Being in the retail scrapbooking market since it began has put us in a unique position to watch scrapbooking develop.

We know scrapbookers are always looking for a new look, a fresh technique or the very latest papers. **Making Terrific Scrapbook Pages** reflects the newest, latest and greatest developments in scrapbooking. It showcases vellum papers, a wonderful new product that reached scrappers just last year. We spotlight chalking techniques, which surfaced about 18 months ago; scrappers seem to find new uses for them every day. Page designers are now doing mosaics and collages while they find new looks for favorites like paper quilting and tea bag folding. They ARE a talented group of people!

While it has been exciting to see scrapbooking grow in the United States, it's also been fun to be part of it as it leaps across the "pond" and finds enthusiastic audiences in England, Australia, New Zealand and other lands. We're especially proud to present winners of our web contests (www.paperpizazz.com). No matter where they live, these ladies are on top of the latest in scrapbooking and certainly deserve a place in this **Terrific** book.

Thanks to our talented page designers. In alphabetical order, they are:

- ★ **Amberly Beck**, Lewiston, Idaho
- ★ **Shauna Berglund-Immel** for Hot Off The Press, Inc.
- ★ **Susan Cobb** for Hot Off The Press, Inc.
- ⊙ **Teri Cutts**, Portland, Oregon
- ⊙ **Paris Dukes**, Hillsboro, Oregon
- ★ **LeNae Gerig** for Hot Off The Press, Inc.
- ★ **Amy Gustafson** for Hot Off The Press, Inc.
- ★ **Emily Gustafson** for Hot Off The Press, Inc.
- ★ **Heidi Havens**, Milwaukee, Wisconsin
- ⊙ **Nicola Howard**, Pukekohem, New Zealand
- ⊙ **Joanne Lee**, Cape Elizabeth, Maine
- ⊙ **Tanya Morrow**, Portland, Oregon
- ★ **Debbie Peterson**, Kennewick, Washington
- ⊙ **Jackie Phelps**, New Plymouth, New Zealand

⊙ *contest winner!*

For a color catalog of over 750 products, send $2.00 to **HOT OFF THE PRESS** INC.
1250 N.W. Third, Dept. B
Canby, Oregon 97013
phone 503·266·9102
fax 503·266·8749
http://www.paperpizazz.com

PRODUCTION CREDITS:

President:
- ★ Paulette Jarvey

Vice-President:
- ★ Teresa Nelson

Production Manager:
- ★ Lynda Hill

Project Editors:
- ★ Mary Margaret Hite
- ★ Diane Weiner
- ★ Lee Shaw
- ★ Joan Hibbs

Photographer:
- ★ John McNally

Graphic Designers:
- ★ Jacie Pete
- ★ Carmalee Justis

Digital Imagers:
- ★ Victoria Weber
- ★ Larry Seith

Making
TERRIFIC
SCRAPBOOK PAGES

It's Easier Than You Think

Includes:
- 228 scrapbook pages
- 21 techniques
- 36 ideas with vellum
- 28 chalking designs

From the creators of:
Making Great Scrapbook Pages
Making Wonderful Scrapbook Pages
Making Brilliant Scrapbook Pages
Making Heritage Scrapbook Pages

TABLE OF CONTENTS

SCRAPBOOKING BASICS

There are some terrific things about scrapbooking! You WILL be successful (you only have to please yourself). It uses products we're all familiar with (paper, scissors and glue). And, best of all, you're actually creating your own legacy, one page at a time. Did I mention it's also fun and a wonderful experience to share? It is, and we're sure you'll love it!

Using this book requires no previous experience. We'll show you the ropes and guide you gently along the scrapbooking path. In this chapter, we'll cover the basics of cropping, matting and building a page. Then we'll offer suggestions for making terrific pages and for choosing papers.

Even highly experienced scrappers will find value in seeing one page layout created using different papers. "Same Layout/Different Looks" offers a handy way to expand your page layout repertoire.

So that you can reproduce these album pages, a materials list is by each page. We've used Paper Pizazz™ scrapbooking papers which are sold in books and by the sheet. The book title is in *italics* and the words "by the sheet" indicate if it's available separately.

Want even more layout ideas? See "Four Designers/Same Photos," as four of our Scrapbook Specialists each works with the same photos. We were surprised and delighted with how different the layouts could be. Bet you'll get some good ideas, too.

"Growing a Page" offers 12"x12" album scrapbookers innovative ways to use 8½"x11" papers to create their larger pages. While more and more 12"x12" papers come on the market nearly every day, it's still a fact that there is more to choose from in the smaller size. Even if your favorite paper only comes in 8½"x11", you'll find ways to make it do what you want and fit in your larger album!

Finally, in this chapter have a look at other types of albums. As scrapbookers fill their family albums, many find making a specialized album is the perfect gift or remembrance. This section will offer other types of albums for you to consider—two of them come directly from Hot Off The Press' experience with the loss of dearly loved co-workers.

This chapter is only the beginning. So, new friend, please sit down, pour a cup and journey with us as we explore and share *Making Terrific Scrapbook Pages*!

STEPS TO BETTER PHOTOS

Sometimes the best photo is a straight-on closeup, with the subject centered in the frame. Often, however, shooting from an unusual angle or with a different emphasis makes for a more interesting picture. Consider these looks:

"Shooting down" can make you see a subject in a whole new way.

A photo taken from behind can touch your heart. It's as though you have a window into a private world.

The subject doesn't always have to be in the center of the photo. The mother and baby on one side are no less the center of attention in this great picture!

Try placing the camera below eye level. See how the photo shows the underside of the swing? It makes the girl look as though she's coming right out of the photo!

HOW TO BUILD A PAGE

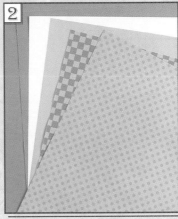

1 Select your photos based on the theme or event for your album page. You might think of each scrapbook page as having a story to tell.

2 Select plain and patterned papers to complement your photos. You may find a themed patterned paper that will mirror the story of your photos. Then choose solid colors to coordinate with the patterned paper. Or you may simply want to choose patterned papers with colors found in your photos. Pages 14–15 offer ideas for choosing and mixing papers.

3 Crop your photos (more about this on page 10). Here a plastic template helps make a perfect circle.

4 Mat your photos on plain or patterned paper (page 11 goes into more detail about matting). Glue the cropped photos to the paper and cut $1/8"$–$1/2"$ away using plain or pattern-edged scissors.

5 Arrange the photos—pages 12–13 will offer some guidelines. Here we've mixed sizes and shapes for a pleasing arrangement.

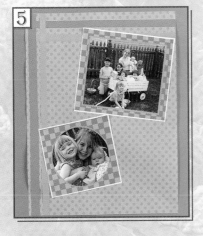

6 Add decorative elements—Punch-Outs™, punches, stickers, die-cuts, etc.

7 Finally, journal. This is where you add the words to finish your page's story. Keep it brief, or make it as complete as you think is necessary.

8 Slip the completed page into a sheet protector, then into your album.

CROPPING

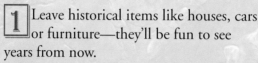

Think of it as clever cutting! Cropping allows you to focus on the important parts of your photos. You can fit more cropped photos on a page, and the pages will be more interesting!

1 Leave historical items like houses, cars or furniture—they'll be fun to see years from now.

2 Trim close to the focal person, place or thing. Use straight or pattern-edged scissors.

3 If you're hesitant about cropping older or one-of-a-kind photos, make a color copy (yes, a color copy is best even for black-and-white photos) and cut the copy for your album page.

4 Use a plastic template for smooth ovals, perfect circles and great shapes. Place the template on top of the photo and draw the shape on the photo with a pencil, then cut just inside the line. Lots of shapes are available.

5 "Silhouetting" is cutting around a person or object. This allows the focal point of the photo to stand out more on your album page. Cut along the edge of the focal point, removing all the background.

6 "Bumping out" is silhouetting one area of a photo, but leaving the rest of the photo with the background. This cropping technique works especially well with elbows, legs and balloons.

7 Don't crop Polaroid photos—if exposed, the chemicals embedded in the layers may cause deterioration of the photo and adjacent page elements. Instead cover the entire photo with a frame cropped to reveal the focal area. (Wait 10–15 minutes for freshly developed photos to dry completely dry before mounting).

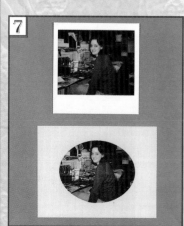

MATTING

Matting is framing a photo or other element with paper to create a visual separation between the photo and the background. It helps the photo "pop" forward off the page.

1 Glue the cropped photo to a sheet of paper and cut ⅛"–½" away, forming a mat. Use plain paper for the mat (see the Golden Rule on page ?). Use straight-edged scissors…

2 …or pattern-edged scissors for one or both cuts. It's fun to mix and match cuts.

3 When matting a bumped-out or silhouetted photo, it's best to keep the mat simple and cut it close to the photo.

4 Double mat some photos. Varying the sizes of the mats from narrow to wide adds interest to the page.

5 Mixing straight-edged and pattern-edged scissors on your photos and mats also adds visual interest.

6 How about a triple mat, just for fun? Or quadruple mat, or more?

7 Mix your mat shapes, perhaps putting an oval inside a rectangle, a circle inside a square or a heart inside a diamond.

8 Journaling on a wide mat makes good use of space and offers a great look!

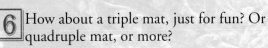

A Few Basic Rules

1 Establish a focal point: The "focal point" is that element on the album page which first attracts the eye. A page without a clear focal point lacks interest. One way to create a focal point is to enlarge one photo and center it on the page—like the top photo in the autumn page at left.

- **patterned Paper Pizzaz™:** fall leaves (*Our Holidays & Seasons*); burlap (*Country*); yellow/brown plaid (*Jewel Plaids* or 12"x12" by the sheet)
- **solid Paper Pizzaz™:** burgundy, brown (*Solid Jewel Tones*)
- **Classic Caps letter template:** Frances Meyer, Inc.®
- **Victorian corner punch:** Fiskars®, Inc.
- **Victorian scissors:** Paper Adventures
- **page designer:** Teri Cutts

2 Vary the photo sizes: Mix photo sizes to add interest to your album pages. The page at left is nicely done, but the right-hand page is more interesting. Sometimes it's a subtle change that makes all the difference.

- **patterned Paper Pizzaz™:** yellow daisies, ivy (*Blooming Blossoms*, ivy also by the sheet)
- **solid Paper Pizzaz™:** yellow, green (*Solid Muted Colors*); black (*Solid Jewel Tones*); white (*Plain Pastels*)
- **scallop scissors:** Fiskars®, Inc.
- **black pen:** Zig®

3 Vary the photo shapes: All rectangles (or all circles, or even all hearts) make for a bland, even boring page. Change the shapes of one or two photos or other elements to provide variety.

- **patterned Paper Pizzaz™:** wildflowers (*Watercolor Florals*); blue dotted vellum (*Colored Vellum Papers*)
- **solid Paper Pizzaz™:** pink (*Plain Pastels*)
- **Punch-Outs™:** butterflies (*Watercolor Punch-Outs™*)
- **silver pen:** Zebra

4 **Overlap elements:** Wonderful things happen when page elements touch and overlap! Not only can you fit more or larger pieces on the page, but the viewer's eye is directed from one element to another in a clear path. The rope pattern is on page 140.

- **patterned Paper Pizazz™:** blue/black plaid (*Jewel Plaids*); blue handmade (*The Handmade Look*)
- **solid Paper Pizazz™:** black (*Solid Jewel Tones*); white (*Solid Pastel Papers*)
- **acid-free chalk:** Craft-T Products
- **black pen:** Zig®

5 **Fill the center:** The center of the page attracts the eye first; if it's empty, the page looks incomplete. Imagine this page without the palm tree. Dull, huh?

- **patterned Paper Pizazz™:** sand (*Textured Papers*)
- **solid Paper Pizazz™:** green, black (*Solid Jewel Tones*); brown (*Solid Muted Colors*); white (*Plain Pastels*)
- **palm tree template:** Provo Craft®
- **starfish template:** StenSource
- **white pen:** Pentel
- **black pen:** Zig®

6 Follow "**The Golden Rule**" for patterned papers: **Mat your photos on plain papers before placing them on patterned backgrounds.** A plain mat visually separates a photo from a patterned background and helps it pop off the page. On this fairly busy pattern, a wide double mat was used to create even more distance.

- **patterned Paper Pizazz™:** fireworks (*Adult Birthday*);
- **solid Paper Pizazz™:** red, blue (*Plain Brights*); yellow (*Solid Muted Colors*); white (*Plain Pastels*)
- **star punch:** Marvy® Uchida
- **wave scissors:** Fiskars®, Inc.
- **deckle scissors:** Family Treasures
- **black pen:** Zig®

HOW TO CHOOSE PAPERS

There is a seemingly endless variety of patterned and solid-color papers to choose from—how do you decide?

Match the clothing color. When you're feeling groovy, only the right period duds will do! The disco colors of this wildly flowered paper match Laura's dress as well as the party mood. Dangling the letters on a punched bead curtain is a playful touch that's echoed around the journaling and photo mats—as though they're draped in love beads.

- **patterned Paper Pizazz™**: disco daisies, bead curtain (*1950s & '60s*)
- **solid Paper Pizazz™**: white, green, peach, pink, hot pink, yellow, gold, purple (*Solid Pastel Papers*)
- **wacky letters template:** Frances Meyer, Inc.®
- **rectangle, triangle, oval punches:** Family Treasures, Inc.
- **¼" hole punch:** McGill, Inc.
- **black pen:** Zig®
- **page designer:** Shauna Berglund-Immel

Match the background colors. These pictures are a natural for the bright colors of the watercolor leaf paper. Picking up the fall colors with wide triple plain colored mats pops the photos away from the background, keeping them the focus of the page. A brown pen was used to keep the look soft.

- **patterned Paper Pizazz™**: fall leaves (*Watercolor Florals*)
- **solid Paper Pizazz™**: burgundy, orange (*Solid Jewel Tones*); ivory (Plain Pastels)
- **Punch-Outs™**: leaves (*Watercolor Punch-Outs™*)
- **deckle scissors:** Fiskars®, Inc.
- **brown pen:** Zig®
- **page designer:** Amy Gustafson

Match the theme or event. The journaling on this page tells a delightful story about how Spencer acquired his fondness for band-aids (journaling on the computer made it easy to fit the whole story in a small area). Every element of the page supports the story, from the background paper to the popsicle and tricycle Punch-Outs™.

- **patterned Paper Pizazz**™: ouch! (*Childhood*);
- **solid Paper Pizazz**™: yellow, red (*Solid Bright Colors*); teal (*Solid Muted Colors*); white (*Plain Pastels*)
- **Punch-Outs**™: tricycles, popsicle, band-aids (*Kid's Punch-Outs*™)
- **spiral punch**: Family Treasures, Inc.
- **black pen**: Zig®
- **page designer**: Shauna Berglund-Immel

Match the emotion. The first day back at school for these college students is a joyous reunion. Before the pressure of studies gets too heavy they're gonna have fun! The youthful, bright colors in the tie-dye paper reflect high spirits and fun. Pulling the mat colors out of the background paper (and varying them for every photo!) just adds to the fun emotion.

- **patterned Paper Pizazz**™: tie-dye, speech bubble (*Our School Days*)
- **solid Paper Pizazz**™: lime, yellow, orange, turquoise (*Plain Brights*)
- **peaks, spindle scissors**: Fiskars®, Inc.
- **black pen**: Zig®
- **page designer**: Amy Gustafson

SAME LAYOUT/DIFFERENT LOOKS

These page pairs share the same layout—sometimes identical layouts—but each has a unique look and feel due to different paper choices, different embellishments and, of course, different photos.

These pages share a layout right down to the bow, yet the left page appears much softer, not only because of the natural elements in the photo, but because of the softer-textured papers. On the right page, the lighter background paper really pushes the photos forward.

- **patterned Paper Pizazz**™: 12"x12" grass (by the sheet); dog bones (*Pets* or by the sheet)
- **solid Paper Pizazz**™: light green, yellow, blue, white (*Plain Pastels*)
- **⅜" wide light blue satin picot ribbon**: Offray
- **cloud, deckle scissors**: Fiskars®, Inc.
- **⅛" hole punch**: McGill, Inc.

- **patterned Paper Pizazz**™: Ho Ho Ho (*Christmas Time*); white dots on red (*Ho Ho Ho* or by the sheet)
- **solid Paper Pizazz**™: dark green (*Solid Jewel Tones*); green, red (*Plain Brights*); white (*Plain Pastels*)
- **⅜" wide light blue satin picot ribbon**: Offray
- **¹⁄₁₆" hole punch**: McGill, Inc.
- **cloud, deckle scissors**: Fiskars®, Inc.
- **page designer**: LeNae Gerig

There's a little more room to spread out on a 12"x12" page, so the designer chose not to overlap the photos—but the layout is substantially the same. The childlike pastels and playful gingham on the left page give it a completely different feel from the vintage elegance of the greens on the other. Deckling the edges of the black-and-white photos and mounting them with photo corners adds to the heritage look.

- **patterned Paper Pizazz**™: pink gingham, pink flowers on yellow (*Soft Tints*)
- **solid Paper Pizazz**™: ivory (*Plain Pastels*)
- **Punch-Outs**™: basket and eggs (*Holidays & Seasons Punch-Outs*™)
- **seagull scissors**: Fiskars®, Inc.
- **black pen**: Zig®
- **page designer**: LeNae Gerig

- **patterned Paper Pizazz**™: green moiré, green tiles (*Heritage Papers*)
- **solid Paper Pizazz**™: black (*Solid Jewel Tones*); ivory (*Plain Pastels*)
- **Punch-Outs**™: postcards (*Heritage Punch-Outs*™)
- **gold photo corners**: Canson-Talens, Inc.
- **camelback scissors**: McGill, Inc.
- **deckle scissors**: Fiskars®, Inc.
- **black pen**: Zig®
- **page designer**: LeNae Gerig

- **patterned Paper Pizazz™**: black tri-dot (*Heritage Papers*); pink tri-dot (*Bold & Bright*); cars, dancers, records, 1950s words (*1950's & 60's Papers*)
- **solid Paper Pizazz™**: aqua, pink (*Plain Brights*); black (*Solid Jewel Tones*)
- **black pen**: Zig® Writer
- **page designer**: LeNae Gerig

Four 5" squares complement the theme and colors of the photo to form the background on each of these pages. A wide central mat offers a journaling space. The Brittney page is clean and zowie-bright, while the Lauren page features rustic tone-on-tone colors and a more muted feel that supports the paler, shadowy colors of the photo.

- **patterned Paper Pizazz™**: frosted leaves, brown plaid (*Great Outdoors*, also by the sheet); fall leaves (*Holidays & Seasons*, also by the sheet); barnwood (*Country*, also by the sheet); red/yellow plaid (*Jewel Plaids*)
- **solid Paper Pizazz™**: black (*Solid Jewel Tones*); white, ivory (*Solid Pastel Papers*)
- **deckle scissors**: Family Treasures, Inc.
- **black pen**: Zig® Writer
- **page designer**: LeNae Gerig

Here we have an "all boy" page contrasted with a very feminine one, because of the colors and the decorative elements. The left page is all geometrics and hard lines; even the deckled mat, normally a subtle edge, is punchy when it's pure white matted on black. The right page features flowing curves and floral patterns—even the squares are scalloped!

- **patterned Paper Pizazz™**: green plaid (*Coordinating Colors™ Jewel Plaids*); green dot on white (*Coordinating Colors™ Hunter Green*)
- **solid Paper Pizazz™**: black (*Solid Jewel Tones*)
- **Punch-Outs™**: school, crayons (*Country Friends Punch-Outs™*)
- **Alphabitties™ sticker letters**: Provo Craft®
- **corner punch, deckle scissors**: Family Treasures, Inc.
- **maxi-cut zig-zag scissors**: Making Memories™
- **mini pinking scissors**: Fiskars®, Inc.
- **page designer**: Debbie Peterson

- **patterned Paper Pizazz™**: lavender and white stripes, lavender speckle (*Lisa Williams Pink, Lavender & Beige*)
- **solid Paper Pizazz™**: burgundy, mauve, olive, sage, gray (*Solid Muted Colors*); white (*Plain Pastels*)
- **Alphabitties™ sticker letters**: Provo Craft®
- **corner, ⅛", ¼" round punches**: McGill, Inc.
- **daisy, square, leaf punches**: Family Treasures, Inc.
- **mini scallop scissors**: Fiskars®, Inc.
- **page designer**: Debbie Peterson

Pool Party at Jamie's

August 2000

Mom and Dad's New Arrival

Millie May born 4-15-99

Jenny and Chris

June 8, 1996

Page corners and wide mats are a classic way to display a large center photo—but how different they look when the triangles are cut from rounded laser lace and the mat is see-through vellum!

Our busy little bee got lots of candy!

Mitchell's First Halloween 1998

"Wallpapering" in panels is a wonderful way to combine patterns and stretch a page. The striped effect is softened on the 8½"x11" page by overlapping daisies (a design pulled from the background paper).

- **patterned Paper Pizazz**™: tie-dye, bright bubbles (*Bright Great Backgrounds*); pool water (*Vacation #2*, also by the sheet)
- **solid Paper Pizazz**™: yellow (*Plain Pastels*)
- **page designer**: Amy Gustafson

- **patterned Paper Pizazz**™: ivy sponged (*A Woman's Scrapbook*); vellum dots (*Vellum Papers*, also by the sheet); laser lace (*Romantic Papers*, also by the sheet)
- **solid Paper Pizazz**™: black (*Solid Jewel Tones*); white (*Plain Pastels*)
- **page designer**: Amy Gustafson

- **patterned Paper Pizazz**™: barnwood, wire & daisies (*Country*, also by the sheet)
- **solid Paper Pizazz**™: yellow, cream (*Plain Pastels*); black, orange (*Solid Jewel Tones*)
- **daisy punch**: Family Treasures, Inc.
- **¼" circle punch**: Marvy® Uchida
- **black pen**: Sakura Gelly Roll
- **page designer**: Amy Gustafson

- **patterned Paper Pizazz**™: candy corn (*Our Holidays & Seasons*, also by the sheet); black with yellow dots (*Bold & Bright*)
- **solid Paper Pizazz**™: yellow (*Plain Brights*); white (*Plain Pastels*); black, orange (*Solid Jewel Tones*)
- **page designer**: Amy Gustafson

Both paper quilted pages were embellished with 2" squares and with triangles made by cutting 2" squares in half diagonally. Less obviously, both pages feature a tone-on-tone effect—achieved on the left page with vellum overlays, and on the right page with papers in different shades of the same color. (Compare the right page with the one at the bottom of page 16 which uses the same green papers.)

- **patterned Paper Pizazz**™: red roses (*Blooming Blossoms*, also by the sheet); laser lace (*Romantic Papers*, also by the sheet); vellum flowers & dots (*Vellum Papers*, also by the sheet)
- **solid Paper Pizazz**™: specialty gold (*Metallic Papers*, also by the sheet); pale yellow (*Solid Pastel Papers*)
- **20" of ¼" wide cream satin ribbon**: Wrights®
- **metallic gold pen**: Zebra Jimnie Gel Rollerball
- **page designer**: Susan Cobb

- **patterned Paper Pizazz**™: green moiré, green tiles (*Heritage Papers*)
- **solid Paper Pizazz**™: sage (*Solid Muted Colors*); pale yellow (*Solid Pastel papers*)
- **Punch-Outs**™: bow charms (*Charms Punch-Outs*™)
- **metallic gold pen**: Zebra Jimnie Gel Rollerball
- **page designer**: Susan Cobb

These pages are identical in layout, each with half-page backgrounds divided by a paper strip and an angled photo on each page half. The colors and textures change the look. Very narrow black mats on the right page separation between the solid and printed pastels.

- **patterned Paper Pizazz**™: green handmade, black handmade, tan handmade (*"Handmade" Papers*); stones (*Textured Papers*)
- **solid Paper Pizazz**™: white (*Plain Pastels*)
- **black pen**: Zig® Writer
- **page designer**: Emily Gustafson

- **patterned Paper Pizazz**™: pastel hearts, pastel stripes, nursery items (*Baby*, also by the sheet)
- **solid Paper Pizazz**™: pink (*Plain Pastels*), black (*Solid Jewel Tones*)
- **Punch-Outs**™: diaper pin (*Baby Punch-Outs*™)
- **black pen**: Zig® Millennium
- **large, small heart punches**: Marvy® Uchida
- **medium heart punch**: McGill, Inc.
- **page designer**: Emily Gustafson

Four Designers/Same Photos

We gave identical sets of photos to four different designers and just turned them loose. As expected, creative minds don't always choose the same path. Just look at the results!

**Molly in her Easter dress
April, 1999**

Amy chose two of the four photos for an 8½"x11" page. She reinforced the dance theme introduced in the lower photo with a clever laced-up sheer "stocking" (a 2½"x11" strip of patterned vellum), then echoed the tulips in the upper photo with a balancing stamp at the lower left.

- **patterned Paper Pizazz™**: dance (by the sheet); vellum swirls (*Vellum Papers*, also by the sheet)
- **solid Paper Pizazz™**: yellow, pink, white (*Plain Pastels*); black (*Solid Jewel Tones*)
- **tulip stamp**: Rubber Stampede, Inc.
- **embossing stamp pad**: Top Boss
- **black embossing powder**: Stampendous!®
- **yellow, green, brown chalk**: Craf-T Products
- **⅛" wide satin ribbon**: C.M. Offray & Son, Inc.
- **foam mounting tape**: Scotch® Brand
- **page designer**: Amy Gustafson

"Sugar and spice & all things nice." Susan has selected two photos that show more of Molly's "spice" side (look closely; you'll see she's sticking her tongue out in the lower photo) to make a bright, fun page embellished with sassy Punch-Out™ faces. Notice Susan cleverly used two patterned papers with similar designs in different sizes.

- **patterned Paper Pizazz™**: pink check, pink gingham (*Soft Tints*)
- **solid Paper Pizazz™**: pale yellow, pink (*Plain Pastels*)
- **Punch-Outs™**: faces (*Punch Art Punch-Outs™*)
- **heart die-cut**: Accu/Cut® Systems
- **black pens**: Zig® Writer
- **page designer**: Susan Cobb

heart © & ™ Accu/Cut® Systems

The only designer to use all four photos, Shauna has fanned three overlapping across the top of the page to save space. She has chosen to emphasize the garden setting of the page with raised flowers and a chalked fence. Notice the carefully drawn lace edge which unites all four photos and the journaling plaque.

- **patterned Paper Pizazz**™: pink diagonal stripe, soft pansies *(Soft Florals & Patterns)*; vellum flowers & dots *(Vellum Papers,* also by the sheet)
- **solid Paper Pizazz**™: pale yellow, white *(Plain Pastels)*; olive *(Solid Muted Colors)*
- **fence die cut**: Accu/Cut® Systems
- **green chalk**: Craf-T Products
- **mini-scallop scissors**: Fiskars®, Inc.
- **green pen**: Zig® Writer
- **foam mounting tape**: Scotch® Brand
- **page designer**: Shauna Berglund-Immel

fence © & ™ Accu/Cut® Systems

doll © & ™ Accu/Cut® Systems

LeNae had so much fun making a little paper doll with Molly's hairdo, then dressing it in pink with a gathered tulle skirt! Simple penwork on the scalloped border and punched flowers are another artistic touch that was easy to do but adds pizazz.

- **patterned Paper Pizazz**™: pink lattice *(Soft Florals & Patterns)*; green stripe and pink flowers *(Soft Tints)*
- **solid Paper Pizazz**™: white, pink, tan, green *(Plain Pastels)*; brown *(Solid Muted Colors)*
- **paper doll die cut**: Accu/Cut® Systems
- **9"x3"** white tulle, needle, white thread
- **leaf, flower punches**: Family Treasures, Inc.
- **fat caps letter template**: Frances Meyer, Inc.®
- **scallop edge ruler**: C-Thru® Ruler Co.
- **pink chalk**: Craf-T Products
- **seagull scissors**: Fiskars®, Inc.
- **white pen**: Pentel Milky Gel Roller
- **black pen**: Zig® Millennium
- **page designer**: LeNae Gerig

**Dick, Jim & Cole in the workshop
1998**

LeNae focused on the masculine environment of workshop and tools, designing a whole set of paper pieced tools to create a border. She chose wood, plaid and solid papers to reinforce the masculine effect. The patterns for the tools, boat and peg captain are on page 141.

- **patterned Paper Pizazz**™: barnwood (*Country*, also by the sheet); red/blue plaid (*The Great Outdoors*)
- **solid Paper Pizazz**™: white, ivory (*Plain Pastels*); navy blue, gray, black (*Solid Jewel Tones*)
- **fat caps alphabet template**: Frances Meyer, Inc.
- **deckle scissors**: Family Treasures, Inc.
- **white pen**: Pentel Milky Gel Roller
- **black pen**: Zig® Writer
- **page designer**: LeNae Gerig

Shauna's page emphasizes the nautical theme of the boat. She used red, white and blue colors, stars and stripes, and a string of jaunty pennants across the page top. She cropped the lower photo in a circle and surrounded it with "ship's wheel" spokes made from square and egg punches.

- **patterned Paper Pizazz**™: blue stripes, blue hollow dots (*Perfect Pairs*™ *Red & Navy*, blue stripes also in *Heritage Papers*)
- **solid Paper Pizazz**™: black (*Solid Jewel Tones*)
- **egg, square punches**: Marvy® Uchida
- **star punch**: Family Treasures, Inc.
- **14" of ¼" ivory rope braid**
- **white pen**: Pentel Milky Gel Roller
- **foam mounting tape**: Scotch® Brand
- **page designer**: Shauna Bergland-Immel

Like LeNae on page 22, Susan takes us right into the workshop. However, she's opted to use a paper with an all-over pegboard pattern and a printed border of tools for a "ten-minute page" that still looks terrific. The screw tops drawn on the corners of the mats and the top plaque add a cute touch and match the toolbox in the corner.

- **patterned Paper Pizazz™**: tools (*Border Papers*)
- **solid Paper Pizazz™**: red (*Plain Brights*); black (*Solid Jewel Tones*)
- **black pen**: Zig® Writer
- **page designer**: Susan Cobb

Amy also sets sail with a sea-going theme, but rather than Shauna's bright red, white and blue, Amy has chosen soft, watery colors. Three layers of wave-edged, swirly green vellum make quite a believable ocean! Tucking the boat into the waves adds to the feeling of motion, and tidy white mats on each photo, mat, wave and boat section keep everything crisply ship-shape.

- **patterned Paper Pizazz™**: bright blue plaid, red/yellow plaid, yellow checked (*Bright Tints*); light blue striped (*Soft Tints*); teal swirls vellum (*Colored Vellum Papers*, also by the sheet)
- **solid Paper Pizazz™**: white (*Plain Pastels*)
- **½" and ½" circle punches**: Marvy® Uchida
- **wave scissors**: Fiskars®, Inc.
- **page designer**: Amy Gustafson

Sara gets flowers from Keith 1998

"LeNae the Knife" jumped at the chance to do some fancy cutting! First she used an oval template to cut a window in the center of the floral paper, cutting around a few roses so they'd extend into the window. She backed the page with handmade purple and slipped a matted photo in halfway. Then she overlapped it with flowers cut from the removed oval and attached with foam tape for a dimensional look.

- **patterned Paper Pizazz™**: roses on black (*Watercolor Florals*); purple handmade ("*Handmade" Papers*)
- **solid Paper Pizazz™**: black (*Solid Jewel Tones*); peach (*Solid Muted Colors*)
- **X-acto® knife** and cutting surface
- **oval template**: Provo Craft®
- **foam mounting tape**: Scotch® Brand
- **white pen**: Pentel Milky Gel Roller
- **page designer**: LeNae Gerig

envelope pattern:
Trace with dashed line on fold of tracing paper; unfold and trace onto vellum. Fold on the solid lines and glue.

Shauna loves collages. Using the patterned collage paper gave her a start, but she also brought in handmade mulberry paper (torn for a halo effect), vellum, silver paper, metallic thread and multi-colored mounting corners. Keeping everything in the color range established by the photo flowers gives the page a together look in spite of the many varied elements.

- **patterned Paper Pizazz™**: pink & purple roses (*Collage Papers*); pink, purple vellum (*Pastel Vellum Papers*)
- **solid Paper Pizazz™**: specialty silver (*Pearlescent*, also by the sheet)
- **green mulberry paper**
- **Punch-Outs™**: key (*Charms Punch-Outs™*)
- **metallic silver pen**: Marvy® Gel Roller
- **foam mounting tape**: Scotch® Brand
- **metallic gold thread**
- **photo corners**: Canson-Talens, Inc.
- **page designer**: Shauna Berglund-Immel

- **patterned Paper Pizazz™**: floral/hummingbird paper (*Bj's Gold & Handpainted Papers*); gold, pink vellum (*Pastel Vellum Papers*)
- **solid Paper Pizazz™**: gold (*Metallic Papers*, also by the sheet); white (*Plain Pastels*)
- **metallic gold pen**: Sakura Gelly Roll
- **page designer**: Susan Cobb

Both Susan and Amy have chosen to highlight a single photo. Susan's idea (right) was to center the photo on the bottom of a gorgeous floral paper, then surround it with a frame of pink vellum. The gold in the background paper is echoed in the gold mat.

Amy picked up the bouquet colors with a mat of pastel plaid, then matted it on plain vellum, scalloped the edges, and outlined the scallops with a white gel pen to match the look of the scalloped edges on the lace background paper. A final plaid mat frames the entire page.

- **patterned Paper Pizazz™**: morning glory lace ("*Lace*" *Papers*, also available by the sheet); multi-colored plaid (*Pastel Plaids*)
- **solid Paper Pizazz™**: white (*Plain Pastels*); plain vellum (*Vellum Papers*)
- **large heart punch**: McGill, Inc.
- **small heart punch**: Marvy® Uchida
- **scallop scissors**: Fiskars®, Inc.
- **white pen**: Pentel Milky Gel Roller
- **black glitter pen**: Sakura Gelly Roll
- **page designer**: Amy Gustafson

**Dave & Spencer playing with the dogs
August, 1999**

A page full of love! To match the coat of the dog in the foreground, Amy used an animal-fur print for the "PUPPY" letters and a black/white plaid for the background. The red for the "LOVE" letters matches the mats, and the letters themselves form bold page borders. Cropping in a heart shape very close to the father and son focuses your attention on the shared love, which hasn't all gone to the dogs!

- **patterned Paper Pizazz**™: white dot on red (*Ho Ho Ho*, also available by the sheet); black/white plaid (available by the sheet); animal fur (*Wild Things*)
- **solid Paper Pizazz**™: white (*Plain Pastels*); black (*Solid Jewel Tones*); red (*Plain Brights*)
- **letters die cuts**: Accu/Cut Systems®
- **foam mounting tape**: Scotch® Brand
- **page designer**: Amy Gustafson

Interestingly, Susan chose the same two photos and the same color scheme for her page—even some of the same papers! The diagonal balance of the page and the framed pet prints paper give it a different look and feel.

- **patterned Paper Pizazz**™: pet prints (*Pets*, also by the sheet); white dot on red (*Ho Ho Ho*, also by the sheet)
- **solid Paper Pizazz**™: red (*Plain Brights*); black (*Solid Jewel Tones*)
- **Punch-Outs**™: dog, doghouse (*Punch Art Punch-Outs*™)
- **white pen**: Pentel Gel Roller
- **black pen**: Zig® Writer
- **page designer**: Susan Cobb

A background paper full of frolicking pets and a die-cut puppy, colored to match one from the patterned sheet, make great go-togethers. Shauna matted her photos and heart journaling plaque to match the border strip on the top and bottom of the paper for a look that is unified top to bottom.

- **patterned Paper Pizazz**™: Love That Pet! (*Annie Lang's Heartwarming Papers*)
- **solid Paper Pizazz**™: blue, white, pink (*Plain Pastels*); black (*Solid Jewel Tones*); green (*Plain Brights*)
- **puppy die cut**: Accu/Cut Systems®
- **heart, bone punches**: Marvy® Uchida
- **mini-scallop scissors**: Fiskars®, Inc.
- **blue, pink, gray chalks**: Craf-T Products
- **white pen**: Pentel Milky Gel Roller
- **black, red pens**: Zig® Writer
- **page designer**: Shauna Berglund-Immel

puppy © & ™ Accu/Cut® Systems

Using a dark background paper pops the wide pet prints paper mats forward; notice one is offset. The smaller photo and dark paw print become embellishments, rather than the main focus. Turning the mats for the separate letters in different directions is a fun touch completely appropriate for the wacky feel of the template letters. The paw print pattern is on page 26.

- **patterned Paper Pizazz**™: blue tri-dots (*Stripes, Checks & Dots*); pet prints (*Pets*, also by the sheet)
- **solid Paper Pizazz**™: black (*Solid Jewel Tones*)
- **wacky letters template**: Frances Meyer, Inc.®
- **metallic silver pen**: Pentel Gel Roller
- **page designer**: LeNae Gerig

GROWING A PAGE

Many scrapbookers prefer larger albums which hold 12"x12" papers—but the paper selection is greater in 8½"x11" papers. So that you have ways to use whatever papers you like no matter what size they come in, here are some ideas for "growing" smaller papers to make large pages.

Cut the 8½"x11" barnwood paper in half lengthwise, then fold the top corners in to meet at the center cut. Cut just below the corners, then cut along the folds to make four triangles. Glue the corners to the 12"x12" ivy sheet. Use the rest of the barnwood to mat a photo and a journaling plaque. Penwork on the barnwood is a nice touch.

- **patterned Paper Pizazz™**: sponged ivy (*Spattered, Crackled, Sponged*); barnwood (*Country*, also by the sheet)
- **solid Paper Pizazz™**: dark green, brown (*Solid Muted Colors*)
- **deckle scissors:** Family Treasures, Inc.
- **white pen:** Pentel Milky Gel Roller
- **black pen:** Zig® Writer
- **page designer:** LeNae Gerig

Yes, it's really blue vellum—one of the neatest things about vellum is how it changes color on different backgrounds! This 8½"x11" blue vellum turns green on yellowish-tan "handmade" paper. These page corners were made like those above, but they were edged with a checked strip for a sharper contrast. The remaining vellum was edged to match and glued diagonally in the center of the sheet.

- **patterned Paper Pizazz™**: blue vellum swirl (*Colored Vellum*); black/white check (*Making Heritage Scrapbook Pages*); tan handmade (*The Handmade Look*)
- **solid Paper Pizazz™**: white, ivory (*Plain Pastels*); blue-green (*Solid Muted*)
- **deckle scissors:** Family Treasures, Inc.
- **black pen:** Zig® Writer
- **page designer:** LeNae Gerig

An easy way to use an 8½"x11" is to cut it into panels. Classic Christmas colors, an elegant red-on red stripe and symmetrical decorations make a holiday page that's traditional, but hardly boring! Splitting the 8½"x11" red stripe into one 3" and two 2½" panels, then matting them separately, lets the paper fill the page. The gold and silver penwork adds a festive touch.

- **patterned Paper Pizazz™**: pine boughs (*Christmas Time*, also by the sheet); red stripe (*Making Heritage Scrapbook Pages*)
- **solid Paper Pizazz™**: black (*Solid Jewel Tones*); ivory (*Plain Pastels*)
- **ornament punch**: Family Treasures, Inc.
- **metallic gold and silver pens**: Pentel Gel Rollers
- **gold metallic calligraphy pen**: Sakura Calligrapher
- **page designer**: LeNae Gerig

The 8½"x11" snowflake paper isn't big enough to fill this page vertically, much less diagonally, but LeNae made it work by cutting it in half lengthwise. She overlapped the ends in the center of the velvet page and trimmed the outer ends even with the corners, then hid the seam with Punch-Outs™. Nicely done!

- **patterned Paper Pizazz™**: snowflake (*Lovely & Lacy Papers*); blue velvet ("*Velvet*" *Backgrounds*)
- **solid Paper Pizazz™**: white, light blue (*Plain Pastels*); navy blue (*Solid Jewel Tones*)
- **Punch-Outs™**: snowflakes (*Lovely & Lacy Punch-Outs™*)
- **deckle scissors**: Family Treasures, Inc.
- **navy blue pen**: Sakura Gelly Roll
- **page designer**: LeNae Gerig

Like the paneled Christmas page on page 29, this one features a single 8½"x11" sheet cut apart and matted separately to give it more visual space. The wide mats in colors pulled from the background dots not only help to add size to the rectangles, but also offer a space for decorative penwork. Notice that the rectangular photo and the journaling plaque in the opposite corner have been glued at different angles to avoid having too many straight and even lines. Stickers overlap in the middle circle.

- **patterned Paper Pizazz**™: scrapbooking (*Annie Lang's Heartwarming Papers*); dots on red (*Great Backgrounds*, also by the sheet*)
- **solid Paper Pizazz**™: black (*Solid Jewel Tones*); blue, green (*Plain Brights*)
- **stickers**: scrapbook angels (*Annie Lang's School Time Stickers*)
- **black pen**: Zig® Millennium
- **mini scallop scissors**: Fiskars®, Inc.
- **page designer**: LeNae Gerig

Making the most of a special 8½"x11" paper (shown below), LeNae has "used everything but the squeal." The borders were cut out to frame the stars page, with star punches filling the empty spaces where they don't quite meet. The center pink area was used for mats, punches and letters, and the stork plaque was matted separately to give it more emphasis.

- **patterned Paper Pizazz**™:"Children are…" (*Janie Dawson's Delightful Companions*); blue stars (*Birthday Time*)
- **solid Paper Pizazz**™: pink, white, yellow(*Plain Pastels*)
- **fat caps, fat lower case letter emplates**: Frances Meyer, Inc.®
- **medium, small star punches**: Family Treasures, Inc.
- **mini scallop scissors**: Fiskars®
- **black pen**: Zig® Writer
- **page designer**: LeNae Gerig

Simple panels are one of the easiest and most effective ways to add page interest. Border strips get extra pizazz when they're cut with pattern-edged scissors—just turn the scissors upside down and align the cuts to make a mirror image. The "Hollywood lights" are simple punches glued into the rounded areas of the borders.

- **patterned Paper Pizazz**™: light blue Mickey balloons, tone-on-tone green Mickey (*Mickey Mouse Simple Backgrounds*)
- **solid Paper Pizazz**™: pink, lavender, yellow, light blue, green (*Plain Brights*); ivory (*Solid Pastel Papers*)
- **Punch-Outs**™: Minnie Mouse (*Disney's Mickey and Friends Punch-Outs*™)
- **¼" hole punch**: McGill, Inc.
- **seagull scissors**: Fiskars®, Inc.
- **black pen**: Zig® Writer
- **page designer**: LeNae Gerig

Disney characters ©Disney Enterprises, Inc.
Used by permission from Disney Enterprises, Inc.

Cut the borders off a background sheet and offset them on a small-patterned or solid paper to expand a page gracefully. The Punch-Out™ journaling and the balancing Pooh figure in the opposite corner create a strong diagonal that carries your eye to the photos between them.

- **patterned Paper Pizazz**™: purple with black dots (*Bold & Bright* or by the sheet); winter fun (by the sheet)
- **solid Paper Pizazz**™: lavender, yellow (*Plain Pastels*)
- **Punch-Outs**™: marching Pooh (*Pooh Punch-Outs*™); letters (*Pooh ABC Punch-Outs*™)
- **deckle, ripple scissors**: Fiskars®, Inc.
- **page designer**: LeNae Gerig

Disney characters ©Disney Enterprises, Inc.
Used by permission from Disney Enterprises, Inc.

The 8½"x11" playground paper (shown below) is cut apart and used in several ways. Cut the letters from the grassy bottom, then mat as many photos as you can with the remaining grass. Use the top to decorate the bottom of the 12"x12" page.

- **patterned Paper Pizzazz™**: hearts, coils and stars (*Childhood Memories*, also by the sheet)
- **solid Paper Pizzazz™**: blue, red, yellow (*Plain Brights*)
- **Punch-Outs™**: ball, pail (*Kids Punch-Outs™*)
- **alphabet template**: Pebbles Inc.
- **black pen**: Zig® Writer
- **page designer**: LeNae Gerig

Everything's coming up (yellow) roses! The 12"x12" yellow roses paper forms the background sheet. The envelope was made from the all-over rose sheet (see the pattern on page 142). The border sheet was used to mat the photo, then the plain side was used to cut the heart (the pattern is on page 35). An extra rose was cut out to embellish the heart. The remaining plain area and the ivory and white papers were used to write various love letters to tuck into the envelope. Wow!

- **patterned Paper Pizzazz™**: yellow roses (*Very Pretty Papers*, also by the sheet); yellow roses with border, yellow roses with all-over pattern (*Watercolor Florals*)
- **solid Paper Pizzazz™**: ivory, white (*Plain Pastels*)
- **envelope die cut**: Accu/Cut® Systems
- **deckle scissors**: Family Treasures, Inc.
- **black pen**: Zig® Writer
- **page designer**: LeNae Gerig

Measure 8" each way from one corner of an 8½"x11" paper, then cut between the points to make a 12"x6" flap. Lining it with cream trimmed in a pretty scallop makes it look like a lovely wedding hankie draped over the page top. The individual roses are cut from the extra roses paper. Artistic effects can be achieved by cutting a die cut like this rose in multiple papers, then cutting them apart and layering them as shown.

- **patterned Paper Pizazz™**: cream roses (*Wedding*, also by the sheet); peach moiré (*Pretty Papers*, also by the sheet)
- **solid Paper Pizazz™**: ivory, white, pink (*Solid Pastel Papers*); sage (*Solid Muted Colors*); black (*Solid Jewel Tones*)
- **rose die cut**: Ellison® Craft & Design
- **long scallop scissors**: Fiskars®, Inc.
- **white pen**: Pentel Milky Gel Roller
- **metallic gold pen**: Pentel Gel Roller
- **black pen**: Zig® Writer
- **page designer**: LeNae Gerig

rose © & ™ Ellison® Craft & Design

As easy as can be: Trim the barnwood paper to 7½"x9½" and mat it on black for a photo background. Cut 1¼"x1⅜" barnwood pieces to mat the letters and apply with foam tape. Add photos and a journaling plaque and voilá! Quite striking.

- **patterned Paper Pizazz™**: beach pebbles (by the sheet); barnwood (*Country*, also by the sheet)
- **solid Paper Pizazz™**: specialty gold (*Metallic Papers*, also by the sheet); black, brown (*Solid Jewel Tones*)
- **fat caps letter template**: Frances Meyer, Inc.®
- **foam mounting tape**: Scotch® Brand
- **deckle, deckle wide scissors**: Fiskars®, Inc.
- **black pen**: Zig® Writer
- **page designer**: LeNae Gerig

OTHER KINDS OF ALBUMS

Theme albums can be just a few pages long, or whole albums centered around a special vacation, a school career, a family history, or any other subject close to your heart.

Heidi set out to capture the special relationship between her husband and their son. This is an ongoing album, with each page featuring an everyday or special event shared by the two. Ben takes great pride in "reading" his book. His dad? Tom cherishes his son's reaction.

- **patterned Paper Pizazz**™: blue swirl, green dots, red check, yellow check, blue stripe (*Bright Tints*)
- **solid Paper Pizazz**™: white, light blue, aqua (*Plain Pastels*); green (*Plain Brights*)
- **Punch-Outs**™: butterfly, headstand, ball & glove, snail, sleepytime (*Annie Lang's Annie's Kids Punch-Outs*™)
- **gold photo corners**: Canson-Talens, Inc.
- **small circle punch**: Family Treasures, Inc.
- **¼" circle punch**: McGill, Inc.
- **black pen**: Zig® Writer
- **album designer**: Heidi Havens

All children love to hear the stories of how they came to be. Adopted children and their new parents often don't have a "birth story" to include in their baby albums. Let the story of the first time you saw your new child be his or her birth story, and tell the exciting details over and over again each time you look at this special storybook album.

- **patterned Paper Pizazz™**: pink moiré (*Wedding*, also by the sheet); yellow dots (*Soft Tints*); pink/yellow plaid (by the sheet); bright floral (*Watercolor Florals*)
- **solid Paper Pizazz™**: white, blue, green, pink (*Plain Pastels*)
- **Punch-Outs™**: flowers, border (*Watercolor Punch-Outs™*)
- **deckle, seagull scissors**: Family Treasures, Inc.
- **black pen**: Zig® Writer
- **album designer**: LeNae Gerig

THE CALL
We had waited for so long to hear news, and then we got the call. It was April 3, 1988 when we received a call from our Case Worker, Jean Thomson. They had a baby girl and would we like to come and look at her! Look at her! We didn't care what you looked like, we knew we were going to bring you home with us. We drove to the Case Worker's office and there in the parking lot we saw you for the first time. You were in the backseat of a Honda in a very big car seat. A woman took you out of the car and carried you inside the building. I knew right then that it was you and I started to cry. Your Dad said, "Don't start crying yet, wait until we get inside."
They left us alone with you for a few minutes to get to know you a little bit, but we couldn't wait to get out of there and get you home. They wanted to know how much history we wanted to know about you. We talked about your health, background and your birth parents. When you are old enough we will tell you everything we know.

You were a happy, healthy, 1 month old, Irish-German, blond baby girl and we loved you immediately. We took you home to meet your big brother, Sam, and some other family members and friends that had gathered at the house. It was wild! You were hungry, but kept choking on your formula until we discovered that your carrier was not the best place to feed you. I had a house full of relatives and Sam wanted to go to the park. When we finally got organized, things calmed down and we laid you sleeping in your new bed. We finally had our baby girl and our family was complete.

you were such a good sleeper those first few nights you were with us. We were happy that you were resting but we wanted you so we could play with you.

Alesia and Daddy

your name — Alesia first belonged to your father's Aunt. We asked her if we could use the name and she said- yes!

Alesia gift from God april 3, 1978

- **patterned Paper Pizazz™**: 2 sheets of green suede (*Heritage Papers*, also by the sheet); tan stripe (*Collage Papers*)
- **solid Paper Pizazz™**: black (*Solid Jewel Tones*); specialty gold (*Metallic Papers*, also by the sheet)
- **18" of ¾" wide forest green satin ribbon**: Wrights®
- **18" of 2½" wide abaca ribbon**: Wrights®
- **metallic silver, metallic gold pens**: Pentel® Gel Rollers
- **album designer**: LeNae Gerig

An anniversary album featuring "then" and "now" photos is sure to be treasured by the anniversary couple, and by their descendants. Having friends and family write their best wishes directly on the pages make them extra special.

Cut the 12"x12" collage paper in half vertically. Glue half to the outside of each green suede sheet. Cut the green ribbon in half and trim the ends as shown. Mat the photos on black, then sandwich the ribbons between the black mat and a gold mat.

At the anniversary party, instead of a guest book, place gold and silver pens on a table next to the album pages for guests to write their messages. Put out extra sheets of suede or another complementary paper for additional signatures. After the party, place all the sheets in page protectors, then put them in an album to present to the honored couple. What a treasure!

When wendy was our receptionist she always had a smile for me each morning. she was my friend and I will miss her so much.

Wendy & Lynda

CATS, CATS, CATS... I will always remember wendy and her love for kitties. she was so loving and kind to both her animals and friends.

A few years ago, Hot Off The Press lost two employees within a year. Feeling the need to do something, we put together a memorial album for each containing photos and notes of remembrance. Each co-worker wrote on a separate page and LeNae scrapbooked the albums. Doing this not only allowed each of us to contribute something unique to the families of our dear friends, but also gave us the chance to work through our own grief and share precious memories. The families still talk about these deeply valued albums.

For Wendy's album we used:
- **patterned Paper Pizazz™**: rose vellum (*Floral Vellum Papers*); green handmade, mauve handmade (*"Handmade" Papers*)
- **solid Paper Pizazz™**: ivory (*Plain Pastels*)
- **Cut-Outs**: vellum pansies (*Vellum Cut-Outs*)
- **deckle cissors**: Family Treasures, Inc.
- **long scallop scissors**: Fiskars®, Inc.
- **black pen**: Zig® Writer
- **album designer**: LeNae Gerig

FOR JOE

Working with Joe was always entertaining. He was everyones little brother. When you were having a bad day he could always be counted on for a back rub and a positive thought. He will be profoundly missed here at Hot Off The Press.

I have the very best memories of Joe. He made the greatest coffee and loved the office dog, Tasha. You may have known him as your son or little brother, but we came to know Joe as a hardworking man with excellent skills and a thirst to always learn more. I will miss him.

For Joe's album we used:
- **patterned Paper Pizazz™**: blue handmade, drieds on blue handmade (*"Handmade" Papers*)
- **solid Paper Pizazz™**: blue, dark blue (*Solid Muted Colors*); ivory (*Plain Pastels*)
- **green mulberry paper**
- **deckle scissors**: Family Treasures, Inc.
- **album designer**: LeNae Gerig

Plant a
little
love, watch
a miracle
grow.
Summer 2000

beaches

VERSATILE VELLUM

The introduction of acid-free, lignin-free vellum papers has hit the scrapbooking world by storm! First there were clear, plain sheets quickly followed by Paper Pizazz™ patterned white-on-white sheets. They made any plain colored paper into a patterned paper.

Colored vellum sheets offered a rainbow from pastels to dark tones from plain colored vellums to patterned colored vellums. Paper Pizazz™ innovated painted vellum which had four-color images on the clear vellum. Painted vellum magically transformed to match any colored paper put under it and went on to create spectacular results with patterned paper under it (see pages 41 and 42).

Now we have heritage vellum, floral vellum, 12"x12" vellum, vellum cut-outs to embellish any page and even metallics on vellum. What a terrific toy box! This chapter focuses on many of the things especially suited to vellum. You'll find frames, paper quilting, tea bag folding, borgello, rubber stamping, dry embossing, matting, growing a page, layering and paper piecing. Whew!

Warning: Vellum is very brittle and any creases will leave a permanent mark. Be careful when purchasing vellum by the sheet to keep it flat. Buying a vellum collection in a book will help protect your purchase.

Scrapbookers question what glue will remain invisible under vellum. We've been most successful with stick glue (acid-free, of course). For perfect results hide the glue whenever possible. For instance, put glue under your matted photo to attach the photo to vellum. Then to attach the vellum to a background sheet, again put glue under the photo—since the finished page goes into a sheet protector you don't have to put glue around the edges of the vellum to secure it. If this seems involved, read the top of page 41 and that should help.

Vellum is terrific and you'll be delighted as you discover its many uses. Be sure to play with it—experiment with different plain and patterned papers under any of the available vellums. Bet you'll love the results!

Vellum, chalking and stamping—all on one page! The photo was reprinted in black & white then chalked. It was triple-matted sandwiching the starburst paper between two narrow layers of white. Both pieces are then glued to the purple vellum whose color ties everything together. A white sheet is randomly stamped and the journaling paper shares the same stamped and embossed image. Two holes are punched 1" apart through the vellum and white sheets. The ribbon is used to hold both sheets together.

- **patterned Paper Pizazz™**: purple starbursts (*Light Great Backgrounds); purple hollow dot vellum (*Colored Vellum Papers*)
- **solid Paper Pizazz™**: white (*Solid Pastel Papers*)
- **mini-victorian scissors**: Provo Craft®
- **flower stamp**: HeroArts
- **amethyst dauber duo stamp ink**: Tsukineko Inc.
- **clear embossing powder**: Rubber Stampede, Inc.
- **¼" hole punch**: McGill, Inc.
- **8" length of ¼" wide sheer white ribbon**: C.M. Offray & Son, Inc.
- **blue, purple, pink pastel chalk**: Craf-T Products
- **page designer**: Amberly Beck

A perfect wedding day is reflected in this ever blooming page! The floral arbor in the photo sets the stage for these paper choices. First the photo is triple matted pulling colors from the photo and papers. Pink roses paper is the background and the center of the vellum sheet is cut freeing the butterflies to be moved closer to the bride and groom.

- **patterned Paper Pizazz™**: pink roses (*Floral Papers*); roses and daisies vellum (*Painted Vellum Papers*)
- **solid Paper Pizazz™**: blue, green, mauve (*Solid Muted Colors*)
- **¼" hole punch**: McGill, Inc.
- **milky white pen**: Pentel Gel Roller
- **page designer**: Amy Gustafson

Wedding photos deserve special treatment and vellum papers are a perfect compliment! The pink and green bouquet colors set the stage when choosing these papers. The floral vintage paper is perfect and even more beautiful when matted on each side with gold paper. Framing the perfect photo is a white-on-white vellum that is layered over a red (that's right, red because the vellum will tone it down considerably) sheet. Both sheets are trimmed slightly and a gold sheet is the final frame. Using a gold pen and following the curves of the vellum sheet ties everything together. Two holes are punched through all papers 1" apart and a shoestring bow is tied.

- **patterned Paper Pizazz**™: floral (*Vintage Papers*); rose border vellum (*Vellum Papers*)
- **solid Paper Pizazz**™: metallic gold (*Metallic Papers*, also by the sheet); red (*Plain Brights*)
- ¼" **hole punch**: McGill, Inc.
- **9" length of ¼" wide white satin ribbon**: C.M. Offray & Son
- **gold pen**: Zebra® Jimnie® Gel Rollerball
- **page designer**: Shauna Berglund-Immel

First place in our vacation pages contest! Tanya set the scene with the painted vellum seashells sheet over a barnwood paper (a very clever combination). The sheets were glued centered on the pebbles 12"x12" paper. Beaches is placed on individual rectangles 1"x1¼" with a torn scrap under each template letter. Then they are punched, strung and glued in place. The matted photos are overlapped and die cuts are added. To frame the scene and hold more journaling, simple wooden posts are hand drawn then added. Not only a terrific use of vellum paper, but a great job of growing 8½"x11" papers into a 12"x12" album page. Patterns are on page 140.

- **patterned Paper Pizazz**™: blue/green pebbles (*Great Backgrounds*); seashell vellum (*Painted Vellum Papers*, also by the sheet); barnwood (*Country*, also by the sheet)
- **solid Paper Pizazz**™: light brown, medium brown, reddish brown, beige (*Solid Muted Colors*); ivory (*Plain Pastels*)
- **sand dollar, starfish die-cut**: Ellison® Craft & Design
- ⅛" **hole punch**: McGill, Inc.
- **brown pen**: Zig® Writer
- **blue pen**: Sakura Gelly Roll
- **lettering template**: Frances Meyer, Inc.®
- **25" length of ⅛" wide string**
- **page designer**: Tanya Morrow

Here's another great way to use the seashells painted vellum shown on page 41. Here the vellum is backed by a water paper with wonderful results. It's the perfect backdrop for any water-related photos. Continuing with the water/beach theme, the photo is first matted with plain paper (see The Golden Rule, page 13) then with the sand sheet. The process is reversed on the journaling piece with the addition of a stencil that's been chalked. The vellum seashell cut-outs are the final, finishing touch.

- **patterned Paper Pizazz™**: pool water (*Vacation #2*, also by the sheet); seashell (*Painted Vellum Papers*, also by the sheet); sand (*Textured Papers*)
- **solid Paper Pizazz™**: lilac (*Plain Pastels*)
- **Cut-Outs™**: sea shells (*Vellum Cut-Outs™*)
- **seashell stencil**: American Traditional Stencils
- **pink, purple, brown, green decorating chalks**: Craf-T Products
- **mounting adhesive**: Keep A Memory™ by Therm O Web
- **brown pen**: Zig® Writer
- **page designer**: Susan Cobb

So many wonderful photos are black and white, yet often it's nice to add some color. This old-fashioned vellum sheet provides a good way to keep the tone of the page and add a touch of nostalgia. It is offset on the green textured 12"x12" page and a phrase is written around the edge. Photos are left whole and black photo corners reinforce the heritage look. Marina's name and the year appropriately fill the center of this page.

- **patterned Paper Pizazz™**: green crackled wood texture (*Spattered, Crackled and Sponged*); ivory heritage vellum (*Heritage Vellum*)
- **solid Paper Pizazz™**: ivory (*Plain Pastels*)
- **black photo corners**: Canson-Talens, Inc.
- **black pen**: Sakura Gelly Roll
- **page designer**: Amy Gustafson

Cutting apart a vellum sheet is another way to make it suit your needs whether they are 8½"x11" or 12"x12". Purple is a perfect accent for this little lady yet the page would have been ho-hum with only a matted photo and journaling. The 8½"x11" colored vellum sheet is cut apart to fit the page. Two opposite corners are cut apart and glued opposite on the 12"x12" sheet. The extra vellum is punched to make more embellishments.

- **patterned Paper Pizazz™**: lavender with white dots (*Stripes, Checks & Dots*); burgundy pansy vellum (*Colored Vellum Papers*)
- **solid Paper Pizazz™**: burgundy (*Solid Jewel Tones*); white (*Solid Pastel Papers*)
- **1" leaf punch**: Family Treasures, Inc.
- **page designer**: Amberly Beck

Here's the same colored vellum sheet used in another way with simple paper quilting behind it. Full-sized sheets of the lavender and burgundy papers were cut in quarters, making a piece 5½"x4¼" of each color. The quarter was cut diagonally making two right triangles. Matching the long side of one triangle to the long side of the white background the triangles are glued to opposite corners. A ¼" wide strip of the opposite color is glued along the edge of each triangle. The photo is double matted and the journaling square is turned on edge to be a diamond. Glue the photo and diamond to the vellum then put glue behind the photo to attach the vellum to the paper quilted background.

- **patterned Paper Pizazz™**: burgundy pansy vellum (*Colored Vellum Papers*)
- **solid Paper Pizazz™**: lavender (*Plain Pastels*); burgundy handmade (*Handmade Papers*); white (*Solid Pastel Papers*)
- **page designer**: Susan Cobb

Here's the same paper quilted background using an all-over colored vellum background. With so many vellum choices it would be easy to adapt this layout to many photos.

- **patterned Paper Pizazz™**: lilac and purple floral print vellum (*Colored Vellum Papers*)
- **page designer**: Susan Cobb

Using vellum to fill empty corners is a great idea. Strips of vellum cut to form a design are called bargello and you'll probably find lots of uses for it! A soft pastel quilt paper is a great background for little Brynn. Her photo is matted on cream and again with blue dot vellum then tucked at an angle into the center of the quilt. A purple hollow dot vellum is a perfect compliment to the blue dot. The strips are ⅜", ½" and ¾" wide, notice the strips all vary. The vellum stuffed animals cut-out snuggles into the corner and is offset by the die-cut heart.

- **patterned Paper Pizazz™**: pastel quilt (*Baby*, also by the sheet); purple hollow dot vellum, blue dot vellum (*Colored Vellum Papers*)
- **solid Paper Pizazz™**: pale yellow (*Plain Pastels*)
- **Cut-Outs™**: teddy bear, giraffe, lamb (*Vellum Cut-Outs™*)
- **small heart #2 die-cut**: Accu/Cut® Systems
- **purple pen**: American Crafts
- **page designer**: Susan Cobb

heart © & ™ Accu/Cut® Systems

Vellum makes a perfect frame but the surprise here is that the vellum has an all-over design while it frames a striped paper with another all-over design. Guess it pays to try paper combinations before deciding whether they can or cannot work! Amy cut the vellum into 1¼" wide strips, then glued them to the page edges to make a frame. The photo is triple matted, ending with vellum that matches the frame. Laser lace motifs are cut and glued to each corner. What a beautiful page!

- **patterned Paper Pizazz™**: pink stripes and roses (*Very Pretty Papers*); pink and purple floral print vellum (*Colored Vellum*); laser lace (*Romantic Papers*, also by the sheet)
- **solid Paper Pizazz™**: pink (*Plain Brights*); white (*Plain Pastels*)
- **page designer**: Amy Gustafson

A perfect blend of browns gets a boost from vellum and white touches. Picking up the brown in this sepia photo, both these brown patterned papers and the matching solid browns come in a paper pack called Coordinating Colors™. Notice the photo has six mats (it is darling) with white separating them. The patterned vellum reinforces the leaf in the patterned brown sheet. Brightly colored leaf Punch-Outs™ are subdued by the vellum overlaying them. They are placed in 2" matted brown squares. A wonderfully coordinated page!

- **patterned Paper Pizazz™**: vellum leaves (*Vellum Papers*); brown and white prints (*Brown & White Coordinating Colors™*)
- **Punch-Outs™**: leaves (*Watercolor Punch-Outs™*)
- **deckle scissors**: Family Treasures, Inc.
- **white pen**: Pentel Gel Roller
- **page designer**: Shauna Berglund-Immel

So much innovation is going on in this page that it's hard to capture! First the painted ladybug vellum sheet has a page of yellow roses trimmed to fit inside the thin red frame. The roses are glued offset on the 12"x12" ivy background. Glue is put on the wrong side of the ladybugs and the vellum sheet is attached over the roses (a great way to hide the glue). The checked sheet is cut into one-check-wide strips. Something new, they are glued around the painted vellum sheet. 1" circle punches of the checked paper become ladybug wings on top of a 1" black circle body on top of a ½" black circle head. The antenna are drawn on. One ladybug is in the ivy.

- **patterned Paper Pizazz™**: yellow roses (*Romantic Papers*); red and black check (by the sheet); ivy (*Blooming Blossoms*, also by the sheet); ladybug vellum (*Painted Vellum Papers*, also by the sheet)
- **solid Paper Pizazz™**: red (*Plain Brights*); black (*Solid Jewel Tones*)
- **½" and 1" circle punches**: Marvy® Uchida
- **black pen**: Zig® Writer
- **white pen**: Pentel Gel Roller
- **page designer**: Susan Cobb

Vellum adds a beautiful touch to many pages. Picking up the green and purple from the photo background, Amy selected a distinctive hydrangea patterned paper along with a suede green and moiré purple that both "read" like solid colored papers but add interest and texture. Now that's combining papers like a pro! The vellum lace border was trimmed to fit the photo placing a lace edge on two sides. The sheer ribbon (looking rather vellum-like) wraps up everything!

- **patterned Paper Pizazz**™: purple moiré, purple hydrangeas (*Very Pretty Papers*); forest green suede (*Heritage Papers*, also by the sheet); vellum lace border (*Vellum Papers*, also by the sheet)
- **solid Paper Pizazz**™: white (*Plain Pastels*)
- **1 yard of ¼" wide sheer white ribbon**: C.M. Offray & Son, Inc.
- **black pen** Zig® Writer
- **page designer**: Amy Gustafson

Talk about versatile vellum, here's the proof! Dry embossing is the technique for this pretty page. Place the plain vellum over a brass stencil. Using a stylus, press along the stencil openings. Notice the photo corners are also dry embossed.

- **patterned Paper Pizazz**™: hunter green with hollow dots, hunter green with hearts (*12"x12" Coordinating Colors*™ *Hunter Green*); plain vellum (*Vellum Papers*, also by the sheet)
- **solid Paper Pizazz**™: light green, dark green, white (*12"x12" Coordinating Colors*™ *Hunter Green*)
- **cake stencil**: American Traditional Stencils
- **colonial scissors**: Family Treasures, Inc.
- **page designer**: Amy Gustafson

Vellum makes terrific mats and not a bad snowman, either! Black is an unusual but effective choice for this Christmas page. LeNae made great use of clever matting of her photos and her vellum embellishments are picture perfect. Although the patterns were hand-drawn, the light bulb pattern is on page 48 to make it easy for you.

- **patterned Paper Pizazz**™: red with white dots (*Ho Ho Ho*, also by the sheet); red and white stripe, green with white dots; (*Christmas*, also by the sheet); vellum swirl (*Vellum Papers*, also by the sheet)
- **solid Paper Pizazz**™: orange (*Plain Brights*); white (*Plain Pastels*); gray, black (*Solid Jewel Tones*)
- **deckle scissors**: Family Treasures, Inc.
- **black pen**: Zig® Writer
- **white pen**: Pentel Gel Roller
- **page designer**: LeNae Gerig

Yummy frosting and made with vellum, it's sure to match the color of any cake! This page grew from an 8½"x11" red dots and lines sheet cut in 2" strips. The chocolate cake is from brown suede paper topped with vellum frosting. Confetti, balloon and the candle Punch-Outs™ make quick work of the page since they're pre-matted. This page looks fun and bright, just like the scrapbook specialists in the photo (hi Amy, LeNae, Shauna and Susan)! Find the pattern on page 143.

- **patterned Paper Pizazz**™: confetti (*Birthday Time!*, also by the sheet); red dots and lines (*Bright Great Backgrounds*, also by the sheet); vellum dots and lines (*Vellum Papers*); brown suede (*Black & White Photos*, also by the sheet)
- **solid Paper Pizazz**™: green, yellow, blue (*Plain Brights*); white (*Plain Pastels*)
- **Punch-Outs**™: balloons, confetti and candle (*Celebration Punch-Outs*™)
- **page designer**: Amy Gustafson

How perfect—vellum ghosts! These are made from the hollow dot white-on-white vellum but they could be plain vellum or even pastel colored vellum! These not-very-scary- ghosts float in a friendly way around the photo and it's fun to overlap them.

- **patterned Paper Pizazz™**: black with swirls (*Bright Great Backgrounds*); vellum hollow dots (*Vellum Papers*)
- **solid Paper Pizazz™**: white, tan (*Plain Pastels*); black (*Solid Jewel Tones*)
- **white pen**: Pentel Gel Roller
- **black pen**: Marvy® Uchida Medallion
- **page designer**: Amy Gustafson

For vellum ideas think glass! These Christmas lights are the white kind and as LeNae was taking down her Christmas tree the idea dawned on her. See page 47 where her earlier lights were colored and vellum is the mat. Notice she punched a tree and left the negative space backed by the pine boughs paper—clever LeNae!

- **patterned Paper Pizazz™**: pine boughs (*Christmas,* also by the sheet); red with white dots (*Ho Ho Ho,* also by the sheet); swirl vellum (*Vellum Papers,* also by the sheet)
- **solid Paper Pizazz™**: black, gray (*Solid Jewel Tones*)
- **tree punch**: Family Treasures, Inc.
- **mini antique victorian scissors**: Family Treasures, Inc.
- **black pen**: Zig® Writer
- **page designer**: LeNae Gerig

Anything you can see through can probably be made from vellum. This page features a vellum envelope and punch vellum steam. The laser lace is certainly a lady-like addition to the annual tea party. It's subtle but the teapot and matting paper is a delicate sponged paper perfectly suited to a sit-down tea! The teapot pattern is on page 142. And notice both are edged with a gold pen.

- **patterned Paper Pizazz™**: green sponged, white with pink sponged (*A Woman's Scrapbook*); vellum with tri-dots (*Vellum Papers*); laser lace (*Romantic Papers*, also by the sheet)
- **¾" swirl punch**: Marvy® Uchida
- **teapot die-cut**: Accu/Cut® Systems
- **maroon pen**: Zig® Writer
- **gold pen**: Zebra® Jimnie® Gel Roller
- **page designer**: Amy Gustafson

Speaking of see-through, how about vellum bubbles? Shauna even drew a silver highlight on each bubble and continued the bubble theme into the journaling. Her choice of the purple and pink curls paper evokes the fun mood and emotion of the birthday. Hey Shauna, how about bubbles from bubble gum?

- **patterned Paper Pizazz™**: purple and pink curls (*Great Backgrounds*); purple vellum with hollow dots (*Vellum Papers*, also by the sheet)
- **solid Paper Pizazz™**: lavender (*Solid Pastel Papers*)
- **1¼", 1"circle punch**: Family Treasures, Inc.
- **ABC Tracers**: EK Success Ltd.
- **Border Buddy**: EK Success Ltd.
- **circle template**: Extra Special Products Corp.
- **scallop scissors**: Fiskars®, Inc.
- **pure violet pen**: Zig® Writer
- **silver pen**: Pentel Gel Roller
- **mounting adhesive**: Keep A Memory™ by Therm O Web
- **page designer**: Shauna Berglund-Immel

How perfect, a vellum vase! And isn't it a marvelous way to capture this childhood activity (personally, I got pretty rocks from my sons). This page is one instance where the photo really needs help to tell the story. Obviously the journaling is critical but isn't the vase of flowers just terrific and it needs to be this big. The lace vellum adds a pretty top to the vase. The gold sponged and white moiré paper punched flowers have shading so they're not flat like they would be with plain papers. Using a photo taken from the back makes me want to join the girls in their flower hunt.

- **patterned Paper Pizazz**™: watercolor flower bunches (*Watercolor Florals*); white moiré (*Wedding*, also by the sheet); gold sponged stars (*A Woman's Scrapbook*, also by the sheet); vellum lace border (*Vellum Papers*, also by the sheet)
- **solid Paper Pizazz**™: green, mauve (*Solid Muted Colors*); white (*Plain Pastels*)
- **1" daisy punch**: Family Treasures, Inc.
- **1" sun punch**: Marvy® Uchida
- **¼" circle punch**: Marvy® Uchida
- **page designer**: Amy Gustafson

Along with glass, many clear plastic items can be from vellum. While we really worry about Amy punching out all these little sprinkles AND gluing them in place, this page is a great memory. And how nice to have the recipe around the edge! The pattern for the video cassette is on page 143.

- **patterned Paper Pizazz**™: red with dots (*Christmas Time*); vellum dots (*Vellum Papers*, also by the sheet)
- **solid Paper Pizazz**™: yellow, pale blue, blue, pale green, white (*Plain Pastels*); green, red (*Plain Brights*); black (*Solid Jewel Tones*)
- **¼" rectangle punch**: Fiskars®, Inc.
- **⅛" circle punch**: McGill®, Inc.
- **black pen**: Sakura Gelly Roll
- **red pen**: Zig® Writer
- **metallic silver pen**: Sakura Gelly Roll
- **page designer**: Amy Gustafson

This gumball machine could have used a plain clear vellum sheet but the swirl vellum just adds to the fun of this page. The patterned colorful candies paper is perfect and so much easier than punching and gluing tons of circles. How fun that one gumball is ready to grab out of the opening! The dramatic dot background paper is another touch in keeping with the playfulness of this page. The pattern for the gumball machine is on page 141.

- **patterned Paper Pizazz™**: black with multi-color dots (*Bright Great Backgrounds*, also by the sheet); colorful candies (by the sheet); vellum swirls (*Vellum Papers*, also by the sheet)
- **solid Paper Pizazz™**: red, yellow (*Plain Brights*); white (*Plain Pastels*)
- **silver pen**: Sakura Gelly Roll
- **black pen**: Marvy® Uchida Medallion
- **page designer**: Amy Gustafson

Darian amused himself on the plane ride by learning to blow bubbles!

Glass cookie jars just have to be made of vellum and filled with chocolate chip cookie paper! Using silver paper as an accent to all the great brown chocolate on this page is a terrific choice. Using the vellum lace border gives a nice top edge to the cookie jar. The cookie jar pattern is on page 140. Hum, what other papers can you put in a vellum jar?

- **patterned Paper Pizazz™**: chocolate chip cookie (*Child's Play*, also by the sheet); chocolate chips (by the sheet); specialty silver (*Pearlescent Papers*, also by the sheet); vellum lace border (*Vellum Papers*, also by the sheet)
- **solid Paper Pizazz™**: brown (*"Handmade" Papers*)
- **paper crimper**: Marvy® Uchida
- **silver pen**: Zebra® Jimnie® Gel Rollerball
- **page designer**: Susan Cobb

Angel wings, fairy wings and clouds are terrific made out of vellum! But don't limit yourself to plain vellum, try a pattern like the swirl vellum wings on a swirl vellum cloud all with a silver lining. Isn't the light blue swirls paper perfect? Notice the silhouette cut is exactly along the baby with no background showing. The pattern for the cloud is on page 140.

- **patterned Paper Pizazz™**: light blue swirls (*Light Great Backgrounds*); vellum swirls (*Vellum Papers*, also by the sheet)
- **solid Paper Pizazz™**: specialty silver (*Metallic Papers*, also by the sheet)
- **alphabet template**: Frances Meyer, Inc.®
- **½" star punch**: Family Treasures, Inc.
- **¼" star punch**: McGill, Inc.
- **silver pen**: Sakura Gelly Roll
- **white pen**: Sakura Permapaque
- **page designer**: Amy Gustafson

Angel wings can come from vellum butterflies or vellum dragonflies or from colored vellum papers! This is a great page idea for any loving grandmother or aunt. Each child is silhouette cut and equipped with the appropriate wings.

- **patterned Paper Pizazz™**: mint swirl, peach tri-dots, mint tri-dots, peach with dots, peach/mint plaid (*Light Great Backgrounds*, also by the sheet); dragonfly wings, butterfly wings (*Painted Vellum Papers*); purple lace, blue lace (*Colored Vellum Papers*)
- **solid Paper Pizazz™**: mint, white (*Plain Pastels*)
- **silver and white pens**: Pentel Gel Roller
- **black pen**: Zig® Writer
- **page designer**: LeNae Gerig

And here is one more way to add angel or faerie wings to a photo, rather than silhouette cutting the people. It's a subtle touch but fun to do and fun to watch people discover in your page! Just cut a slit along each side of the person and slip in their wings. Also notice the fine-lined flight paths for the winged things. Nice job!

- **patterned Paper Pizazz™**: gold sponged stars (*A Woman's Scrapbook*, also by the sheet); purple swirl (*Pretty Papers,* also by the sheet)
- **solid Paper Pizazz™**: black (*Solid Jewel Tones*)
- **Vellum Cut-Outs™**: butterflies and dragonflies
- **metallic gold pen**: Pentel Gel Roller
- **black pen**: Zig® Writer
- **page designer**: LeNae Gerig

Pockets are a wonderful use for vellum! You can put flower petals, a lock of hair, invitation, letter or so many things in them. Mat the photo then cut off one of the lace vellum borders and glue it to one edge of your photo mat. Pretty, huh? Then fold the vellum lace border so the other lace edge is on top. The pocket is 4" tall by 4½" wide so the sheet will be 8" tall by 4½" wide. Fold it in half keeping the lace border at the open top. Punch one hole ½" from the fold and another ½" from the pocket opening. Then make three punches between the two. Repeat on the other side. Cut the ribbon in half and thread beginning on the wrong side. Glue the ribbon tail under the pocket and tie a shoestring bow. Glue everything in place.

- **patterned Paper Pizazz™**: purple hydrangeas (*Pretty Papers,* also by the sheet); vellum lace border, heart vellum (*Vellum Papers,* also by the sheet)
- **⅛" hole punch**: McGilll, Inc.
- **20" of ⅛" wide pink satin ribbon**: C.M. Offray & Son, Inc.
- **metallic gold pen**: Marvy® Uchida
- **small heart die-cut**: Accu/Cut® Systems
- **page designer**: Susan Cobb

heart ©Accu/Cut® Systems

Envelopes don't have to be clear, use patterned colored vellum for a new twist! This page certainly has a perfect combination of papers to compliment these photos. The lace paper is trimmed to 10½"x11" and glued to the moiré sheet. The envelope measures 5"x8½" and the flap is the corner of the same vellum sheet which you can put in place and trim to fit. This lovely layout would be perfect for so many photos—like that special one of your mother.

heart ©Accu/Cut® Systems

- **patterned Paper Pizazz™**: burgundy moiré antique lace (*For Black & White Photos*); burgundy pansy vellum (*Colored Vellum Papers*)
- **solid Paper Pizazz™**: beige (*Solid Muted*); deep burgundy (*Solid Jewel Tones*)
- **3" wide heart die-cut**: Accu/Cut® Systems
- **silver photo corners**: Canson-Talens, Inc.
- **metallic silver pen**: Zebra® Jimmie® Gel Rollerball
- **black pen**: Zig® Writer
- **mounting adhesive**: Keep A Memory™ by Therm O Web
- **photography**: INVU Portraits
- **page designer**: Susan Cobb

Layer vellum papers for some wonderful effects. From the bottom: pink moiré, floral vellum (with photo and journaling), plum pink vellum (pocket), floral border vellum (on top of the pocket). The dried, pressed flowers are between the plum pink and floral border vellums. A silver thread was stitched along the edge of the plum pink vellum and a silver pen was used around the journaling heart and the floral border vellum. Pretty pink and flowers are certainly the theme in this page as all eyes are on the charming little girl!

- **patterned Paper Pizazz™**: pink moiré (*Wedding*, also by the sheet); floral vellum (*Floral Vellum Papers*); plum pink vellum (*Pastel Vellum Papers*)
- **solid Paper Pizazz™**: mauve (*Solid Muted Colors*)
- **3" wide heart die-cut**: Accu/Cut® Systems
- **silver metallic thread**: Westrim® Crafts
- **metallic silver pen**: Sakura Gelly Roll
- **mounting adhesive**: Keep A Memory™ by Therm O Web
- **page designer**: Susan Cobb

heart ©Accu/Cut® Systems

Of course, snow globes are perfect made of vellum. And what could be easier (or more appropriate) than a snowman Punch-Out™ inside? To continue the theme, letters are cut from vellum as are the photo corners.

- **patterned Paper Pizazz**™: snowflakes (*Christmas*, also by the sheet); snowflake vellum, tri dot vellum (*Vellum Papers*, also by the sheet)
- **solid Paper Pizazz**™: black (*Solid Jewel Tones*); white (*Plain Pastels*); aqua blue (*Plain Brights*)
- **snowman Punch-Out**™: *Christmas Punch-Outs*™
- **fat caps alphabet template**: Frances Meyer, Inc.®
- **black pen**: Zig® Writer
- **white pen**: Pentel Milky Gel Roller
- **Acid free double stick tape**: Scotch® Brand
- **page designer**: LeNae Gerig

Molly's making bubbles so, of course, her page must have vellum bubbles all over it. But let's use colored vellum so they will really show up! This technique is also called pulling an element from the photo and using it on the page. Scrapbookers do it all the time with paper dolls but you can do it with other things too. To keep the look, Amy used bubble-shaped die-cut letters and cut them from two colored vellums then overlapped them. It's a great look that really captures the spirit of Molly's day.

- **patterned Paper Pizazz**™: yellow with dots (*Stripes, Checks & Dots*); purple hollow dot vellum, blue dot vellum (*Colored Vellum Papers*)
- **solid Paper Pizazz**™: lavender, pale blue (*Plain Pastels*)
- **letter die-cuts**: Accu/Cut® Systems
- **metallic silver pen**: Sakura Gelly Roll
- **white pen**: Sakura Permapaque
- **page designer**: Amy Gustafson

Vellum has other surprises! Susan really hit the mark with this innovation. The purple and blues begin with the flowers in the photo and are echoed all over this page. Choosing the purple sponged paper as a background creates a wonderful starting point that "reads" as a solid. Offsetting the iris painted vellum leaves room for the other flowers. The photo and heart are double matted then finished with a wider mat of stitched lilac vellum. Cut the irises from the last vellum sheet. Use the remaining border to make the bouquet holder. Cut a 5" square and place so it looks like a diamond. Measure 2¾" from one tip and fold it to the center. Repeat with the other side. Then fold each flap over as shown. Add the cut out irises. What a page! The folding diagram is on page 140.

heart ©Accu/Cut® Systems

- **patterned Paper Pizazz**™: purple sponged (*Very Pretty Papers*); 2 sheets of iris vellum (*Painted Vellum Papers*); stitched lilac vellum (*Colored Vellum Papers*)
- **solid Paper Pizazz**™: dark blue, dark green (*Solid Jewel Tones*); ivory (*Plain Pastels*)
- **3" heart die-cut**: Accu/Cut® Systems
- **9" of ⅝"wide lavender satin ribbon**: C.M. Offray & Son, Inc.
- **black pen**: Zig® Millenium Writer
- **page designer**: Susan Cobb

Here's another version of the flower bouquet shown above. Cut around the edge of the painted vellum sheet leaving a ¼" clear border. Then cut the gingham to fit inside the checked border of the sunflower vellum. To hide the glue, glue the gingham to the dotted paper and put glue on the backside of the vellum sunflowers and position the vellum sheet. Cut out the sunflower vellum cut-outs. Cut a 3" square of green vellum and turn it as a diamond with the border at the top. Fold the right corner toward the center, creasing it 1½" from the corner down to the bottom point. Repeat. Fold the corners back as shown and tie with raffia.

- **patterned Paper Pizazz**™: yellow gingham (*Bright Tints*); black with white dots (*Making Heritage Scrapbook Pages*, also by the sheet); painted vellum sunflowers (*Painted Vellum Papers*); green ivy vellum (*Colored Vellum Papers*)
- **solid Paper Pizazz**™: yellow (*Solid Muted Colors*)
- **Vellum Cut-Outs**™: painted vellum sunflower
- **6" of natural raffia**: American Oak Preserving Co., Inc
- **black pen**: Zig® Writer
- **page designer**: Susan Cobb

Vellum is terrific for tea bag folding even though the creases will show. First cut the maroon diamonds, vellum and black papers each into sixteen 1½" squares. Follow the instructions on page 98 to fold eight maroon kites. Glue to the green paper with the long tails pointing out (the edges should just meet). Fold eight black kites then fold them in half and glue on top of the first row as shown. Repeat with eight vellum kites glued in place. Cut a ⅛" wide green mat (also cut out the center of the motif) then mat again making a ⅛" black mat. Repeat to make another tea bag folded motif. The same green vellum is a narrow mat around both photos. Notice the center of the motifs is used for journaling.

- **patterned Paper Pizazz**™: maroon with leaves, maroon diamonds (*Heritage Papers*); green vellum with leaves (*Colored Vellum Papers*)
- **solid Paper Pizazz**™: black (*Solid Jewel Tones*); green (*Solid Muted Colors*)
- **green pen**: Zig® Writer
- **page designer**: Amy Gustafson

Using white-on-white vellum gives a lacy, delicate look to tea bag folding. Two tea bag folds are used on this page. Because vellum softens the color of any paper put under it, a brightly-colored pink roses paper goes underneath the vellum lace border. Cut 12 squares out of roses vellum each 1½" wide. Cut and fold into diamonds, see page 98. Cut the remaining four squares diagonally and fold them into squares, as shown on page 100. Glue as shown to the mauve paper and cut a ⅛" mat also cutting out the center. Repeat making a white mat but do not cut out the center, use it for journaling.

- **patterned Paper Pizazz**™: roses (*Wedding*, also by the sheet); vellum lace border, rose vellum (*Vellum Papers*, also by the sheet)
- **solid Paper Pizazz**™: mauve (*Solid Jewel Tones*); cream (*Plain Pastels*)
- **silver photo corners**: Canson-Talens, Inc.
- **9" of ¼" wide mauve satin ribbon**: C.M. Offray & Son, Inc.
- **metallic silver pen**: Zebra® Jimnie® Gel Rollerball
- **page designer**: Susan Cobb

AUDRIE

Happy First Birthday!
April 3, 2000

1

Let There be Cake!
Kaelin's 1st Birthday party
APRIL 1st, 2000

After fouling out of the game, the only thing Tommy had to look forward to were the oranges at halftime.

CHALKING

Chalks especially made for scrapbooking are another new tool for us. We're particularly fond of Craf-T's decorative chalks which are highly pigmented and they're acid-free. Beware of using artists' chalks which contain oils and can ruin album pages. Fine chalks are brittle but it's easy to use pieces with great results.

Decorative chalks generally come with small sponge applicators which are similar to eye shadow wands. Q-tips® and cotton balls can also be used for applying and blending the chalks.

Like so many things in scrapbooking, once you begin using chalks, you'll find lots of uses for these colorful additions to your pages. In this chapter you'll see chalks used to add contrast and dimension to die-cuts and paper piecing. Chalks can be used to color in stamped images and to add color to copies of black & white photos with charming results. Use them on punched pieces or use them on the negative image left by a paper punch. Finally, at least for now, they can be used on papers to add a specific color or on laser lace. Pretty remarkable versatility for a 1" square of color!

To keep the chalk from migrating to other areas of your page, the manufacturer recommends spraying the chalked areas with a spray fixitive like Blair™ No Odor Spray Fix. Be sure to spray outside because of the fumes.

Chalking die-cut letters is an easy way to make some interesting looks. To achieve this graduated look begin with the applicator at the top of the letter and stroke sideways allowing the chalk to lighten as you move down. Notice the blue chalking is picked up with the blue mats and blue punches. Matting the Dad paper on black provides the separation needed to make this page work.

- **patterned Paper Pizazz™**: dots on red (*Great Backgrounds*, also by the sheet); dad's (*Holiday & Seasons*)
- **solid Paper Pizazz™**: black (*Solid Jewel Tones*); blue (*Solid Bright Papers*); white (*Solid Pastel Papers*)
- **bike punch**: Marvy® Uchida
- **letters**: Accu/Cut® Systems
- **ripple scissors**: Fiskars®, Inc.
- **black pen**: Zig® Millenium
- **blue decorative chalk**: Craf-T Products
- **page designer**: LeNae Gerig

Not only are the letters chalked but so are the die-cut balloons and the edges of the white patterned paper. Orange chalk is used to edge the yellow balloons while blue and green chalks are used on the same-colored balloons. A narrow chalked border rims the die-cut letters while red chalk turns pink when lightly applied around the patterned sheet. What a festive page!

- **patterned Paper Pizazz™**: colorful dots (*School Days*, also by the sheet); dots on red (*Great Backgrounds*, also by the sheet); birthday critters paper (*Genene Cotten's Cute Critters Papers*)
- **solid Paper Pizazz™**: yellow, green blue (*Plain Brights*)
- **red, orange, blue, green decorative chalks**: Craf-T Products
- **black pen**: Zig® Millenium Writer
- **page designer**: Susan Cobb

Chalks can be blended to create a unique look. Amberly first put a ½" wide row of pink chalk applied with a Q-tip® followed by a ½" row of blue with a blank area between the two. With a cotton ball, she blended the two colors until she was pleased with the effect. Then letters were cut out. The sponged background paper picks up the same colors and provides a great background. Vellum strips 2½" wide are a nice touch at the edges. While mulberry paper is not acid-free, Amberly chose to use it. The vellum bubbles have a highlight of chalk around the edge.

- **patterned Paper Pizazz™**: purple sponged (*Pretty Papers,* also by the sheet), hollow dot vellum (by the sheet)
- **ABC tracers**: EK Success Ltd.
- **circle template**: Provo Craft®
- **½" circle punch**: McGill, Inc.
- **pink, blue, purple decorative chalks**: Craf-T Products
- **mulberry paper**
- **mounting adhesive**: Keep A Memory™ by Therm O Web
- **page designer**: Amberly Beck

Chalked circles make cute, funny and charming baby faces! Dot and plaid patterned papers with the same colors are perfect for this page. The plaid strips are 2" wide and triple matted just like the photos. How simply the punched circles are turned into baby faces! With red chalked cheeks and brown chalked edges they perfectly embellish this page.

- **patterned Paper Pizazz™**: pastel dots (*Baby's First Year*); pastel plaid (*Pastel Plaids*); blue moire (*Light Great Backgrounds*)
- **solid Paper Pizazz™**: pink, green, yellow, peach (*Solid Pastel Papers*)
- **letter die-cuts**: Accu/Cuts® Systems
- **1" circle punch**: Family Treasures, Inc.
- **red decorative chalk**: Craf-T Products
- **brown and black pen**: Zig® Writer
- **page designer**: Amy Gustafson

Matthew's second grade Christmas program December 1999

Chalking is a terrific addition to paper piecing. This Santa is darling but the blue chalking around his beard and moustache really give him dimension as does the red chalking around the striped hat. What a good idea to carry the blue chalking around the journaling. The squiggled pen work around the Santa also adds a great touch. Cutting the patterned papers on the diagonal creates a fun, lively page. Santa pattern on page 141.

- **patterned Paper Pizazz™**: red and white stripe, red with white dots (*Ho Ho Ho!!!*, also by the sheet)
- **solid Paper Pizazz™**: red, green (*Ho Ho Ho!!!*); white (*Plain Pastels*); peach (*Solid Muted Colors*)
- **holly punch**: Family Treasures, Inc..
- **1/8" circle punch**: Fiskars®, Inc.
- **blue, red, green decorative chalks**: Craf-T Products
- **black pen**: Zig® Millenium Writer
- **page designer**: Susan Cobb

Chalking, even just a touch, adds depth to die-cuts. The cherry die-cut is cut from red, brown and green papers then cut apart and re-formed to create the pieces you see here. The patterns are on page 141. A swipe of dark green shades the leaves and yellow green highlights the other side of each cherry leaf. On the cherries purple (!) shades them defining their shape with orange and yellow highlights. The elements on Janie Dawson's page are cut apart and reformed as shown—it's a good technique to remember.

- **patterned Paper Pizazz™**: red with hollow dots (*Bold & Bright*, also by the sheet); cherry with checked border (*Janie Dawson's Sweet Companions*)
- **solid Paper Pizazz™**: white (*Plain Pastels*); red, green (*Plain Brights*); black, brown (*Solid Jewel Tones*)
- **cherries die-cut**: Accu/Cut® Systems
- **purple, orange, yellow, dark green, yellow green decorative chalks**: Craf-T Products
- **scallop long scissors**: Fiskars®, Inc.
- **black pen**: Zig® Writer
- **white pen**: Pentel Gel Roller
- **page designer**: LeNae Gerig

Chalk die-cuts cut from patterned or plain papers. Often you'll use the same chalk color as the paper like the brown chalk on the chocolate ice cream and yellow chalk on the gingham cone. This page not only combines two patterns, gingham and swirls, it also uses opposite colors for an eye-catching page. Notice the fun pen work around the white mats.

- **patterned Paper Pizazz**™: lavender and yellow gingham, lavender swirls (*Soft Tints*)
- **solid Paper Pizazz**™: brown (*Solid Muted Colors*); white (*Plain Pastels*)
- **ice cream cone die-cut**: Accu/Cut® Systems
- **scallop scissors**: Fiskars®, Inc.
- **brown, yellow, white decorative chalks**: Craf-T Products
- **plum-mist pen**: Zig® Writer
- **page designer**: Shauna Berglund-Immel

© &™ Accu/Cut® Systems

Chalked paper piecing with a story to tell! Scrappers asked for this spaghetti paper and that first spaghetti dinner is usually a messy affair. Another pair of opposite colors is used here with red and purple, see how effective it is for a fun page. The 2⁷/₈" face and bib circle has ⁷/₈" circle ears and mouth, ¹/₂" nose, eyes and eyelids. Smearing red chalk reinforces the theme of this page.

- **patterned Paper Pizazz**™: spaghetti (*Yummy Papers*); red and white diamonds (*Red and White Coordinating Colors*™)
- **solid Paper Pizazz**™: lavender, brown, ivory, light blue (*Solid Muted Colors*); black (*Solid Jewel Tones*)
- **spiral punch**: Family Treasures, Inc.
- **circle template**: Provo-Craft®
- **letter template**: Provo-Craft®
- **red decorative chalk**: Craf-T Products
- **black pen**: Zig™ Millenium
- **page designer**: Amberly Beck

Experiment with a touch of chalk. In this page chalks are rubbed on the outside photo mat then blended with a Q-tip®. The apple heart is an example of taking an element out of the background paper and enlarging it. This apple has a chalked leaf, center and a touch of brown around the center of the white heart. See the view with the apple opened to tell the story of this dear photo.

- **patterned Paper Pizazz**™: girl with apples (*Annie Lang's Heartwarming Papers*); red moiré (*For Black & White Photos*)
- **solid Paper Pizazz**™: cream, yellow (*Plain Pastels*); brown, black (*Solid Jewel Tones*)
- **heart templates**: Extra Special Products Corp.
- **green, orange, red, yellow, brown decorative chalks**: Craf-T Products
- **black pen**: Zig® Writer
- **page designer**: Susan Cobb

This orange is cut from yellow patterned and yellow vellum papers but it's the orange chalk that turns it into an orange! The die-cut is cut from three papers: squiggled yellow patterned, white and patterned yellow vellum. They are cut apart and re-formed as shown. The orange chalk edges all the pieces. The cloud and grass papers are perfectly joined for this page; notice the grass is cut along the pattern. Another section of grass is cut and the matted photo slipped under it.

- **patterned Paper Pizazz**™: clouds (*Vacation,* also by the sheet); grass (*Pets,* also by the sheet), patterned yellow vellum (*Colored Vellum Papers*); squiggled yellow (*Soft Tints*)
- **solid Paper Pizazz**™: muted yellow (*Solid Muted Colors*); white (*Plain Pastels*)
- **orange slice**: Accu/Cut® Systems
- **orange, red-orange decorative chalks**: Craf-T Products
- **black pen**: Marvy® Uchida
- **foam mounting tape**: Scotch® Brand
- **page designer**: Shauna Berglund-Immel

Use chalk to match a die-cut with patterned paper. These leaves pick up the autumn colors of the background paper with a little help from chalks. Broken lines and dots with the copper pen finish the look. Paris has beautifully combined papers accenting with copper around the photo, as a frame to the whole page and to visually hold the leaves together. Several raffia lengths do a nice job of uniting the leaves with a natural touch. How clever to use a simple ⅝" vellum strip to hold the journaling. Congratulations to Paris for an honorable mention in the Autumn Pages with Pizazz™ contest!

© &™ Accu/Cut® Systems

- **patterned Paper Pizazz™**: frosted leaves (*The Great Outdoors*); copper (*Heavy Metals Papers*); vellum (*Vellum Papers*)
- **solid Paper Pizazz™**: cream, beige (*Solid Pastel Papers*)
- **pop dots**: All Night Media®, Inc.
- **leaf die-cut**: Accu/Cut® Systems
- **four-11" length of raffia**
- **brown, red decorative chalks**: Craf-T Products
- **copper pen**: Sakura Gelly Roll
- **page designer**: Paris Dukes

Chalk can easily shade mats and patterned papers as well as die-cuts. Every paper on this page compliments the theme and feel of the story. The flannel is warm and cozy. The barnwood is very effective as wide photo mats and different parts of the paper are used for the roof and front of the cabin. Brick makes good mats (notice they are one row wide), for the cabin's chimney and as decorative strips at the top and bottom of the page. Shauna used chalks to shade the planks on the cabin as well as to make a shadow on the roof. She also edged the brick mats. It's subtle but makes the page even richer and better. The cabin pattern is on page 142.

- **patterned Paper Pizazz™**: brown flannel plaid (*Flannel Plaid Coordinating Colors™*); 12"x12" brick wall (by the sheet); barnwood (*Country*, also by the sheet); black handmade (*The Handmade Look*)
- **solid Paper Pizazz™**: white (*Plain Pastels*)
- **log cabin die-cut**: Accu/Cut® Systems
- **brown, black decorative chalks**: Craf-T Products
- **black pen**: Marvy® Artist
- **page designer**: Shauna Berglund-Immel

Sleep baby sleep

Counting Sheep

June 2000

What a great way to count sheep—chalked sheep, of course! Plain colored sheep would be sweet but chalked ones are better. All it takes is dabbing dots of chalk and some easy outlining to give these little guys their charm. A bit of pink chalk at the cheeks is also nice. The die-cut fence is beautifully adorned with lots of punched flowers and green pen vines. Baby Lauren is fast asleep with a plaid mat that matches her blanket. A well designed page! The pattern for the fence is on page 21.

- **patterned Paper Pizazz™**: pink/yellow plaid (*Pastel Plaids,* also by the sheet); 12"x12" clouds (by the sheet); 12"x12" grass (by the sheet)
- **solid Paper Pizazz™**: red, blue, yellow-orange, green (*Solid Brights*); pink, yellow, white (*Plain Pastels);* black (*Solid Jewel Tones*)
- **lamb die-cut**: Ellison® Craft & Design
- **fence die-cut**: Accu/Cut® Systems
- **daisy, small star, small heart, medium flower, small leaf punches**: Family Treasures, Inc.
- **tulip punch**: Marvy® Uchida
- **flower punch**: McGill, Inc.
- **black, white, pink decorative chalks**: Craf-T Products
- **black, green, white**: Pentel Gel Rollerball
- **page designer**: LeNae Gerig

Enhance your journaling as well as die-cuts with chalks. The pink and blue of Kaelin's hat give the colors for this page. It's hard to see her birthday cake in the photo (much of it is on her) so the die-cut needs to set the theme. The cake slice is cut from swirl and ripple papers with chalk shading the outside edges. A penned dot and line outline is repeated on the cake slice, mat and journaling circle. Cross-hatching adds even more shadow over the chalking and it, too is repeated on the mat. Both circles have a chalked swirl that's very effective.

- **patterned Paper Pizazz™**: blue with blue flowers, pink swirls, pink striped yellow ripple (*Soft Tints*)
- **solid Paper Pizazz™**: white (*Plain Pastels*)
- **birthday cake slice**: Accu/Cut® Systems
- **1¼" circle punch**: Family Treasures, Inc.
- **swirl, flower punch**: Marvy® Uchida
- **orange decorative chalk**: Craf-T Products
- **black pen**: Marvy® Uchida Medallion
- **page designer**: Shauna Berglund-Immel

Let There be Cake!
Kaelin's 1st Birthday Party
April 1st 2000

Again, chalking adds depth. Imagine these clouds as plain white papers. They would be okay, but just okay. With a bit of blue chalk around the edges, they look more 3-dimensional. Cut a slit in the sheet protector and slip the top clouds though so you can open them while they're in your album. The cloud pattern is on page 141.

- **patterned Paper Pizazz**™: friends, star papers (*Janie Dawson's Special Companions*)
- **solid Paper Pizazz**™: solid red (*Plain Brights*); white (*Plain Pastels*)
- **light blue decorative chalk**: Craf-T Products
- **black pen**: Zig® Writer
- **page designer**: Susan Cobb

It's fun to play with different colored chalks to see what results you'll get. Shauna used two greens and a yellow. She kept the darkest shade on the outside of the trees and got lighter with yellow closest to the center of each tree. That's shading and highlighting! The pattern is on page 141.

- **patterned Paper Pizazz**™: pine trees (*The Great Outdoors*); starry nights (by the sheet)
- **solid Paper Pizazz**™: yellow (*Plain Pastels*); green (*Plain Brights*)
- **tree border die-cut**: Ellison® Craft & Design
- **moon, star punches**: Family Treasures, Inc.
- **dark green, light green, yellow, orange decorative chalks**: Craf-T Products
- **Funky Journaling Genie**: Chatterbox, Inc.
- **blue pen**: Zig® Writer
- **page designer**: Shauna Berglund-Immel

You can chalk rubber stamped images. Simply stamp the images then use chalk instead of markers. On these images the heaviest chalking is in the center of the leaves and flowers with the color fading toward the outside of each petal or leaf. The white mulberry paper carries the white of the stamped papers and journaling plaque. But remember, mulberry paper is not acid-free.

- **patterned Paper Pizazz™**: burgundy suede (by the sheet)
- **solid Paper Pizazz™**: burgundy (*Solid Jewel Tones*); white (*Solid Pastel Papers*)
- **tulip stamp**: Hero Arts®
- **black stamp pad**: Marvy® Uchida
- **green, burgundy decorative chalks**: Craf-T Products
- **Zig® blender pen**: EK Success Ltd.
- **clear photo corners**: Fiskars®, Inc.
- **deckle scissors**: Family Treasures, Inc.
- **black pen**: Zig® Millenium
- **page designer**: Amberly Beck

Here's more chalked stamping. LeNae combined chalk colors as she completed this image. Purple and pink chalks make the grapes while yellow and orange are used in the glass behind the grapes. The two unequal strips of black paper are a nice backdrop for the stamped image.

- **patterned Paper Pizazz™**: blue/burgundy sponged (by the sheet)
- **solid Paper Pizazz™**: black, burgundy (*Solid Jewel Tones*)
- **stained glass grapes rubberstamp**: Rubber Stampede®
- **black stamp pad**: Clearsnap, Inc.
- **purple, pink, blue, light green, dark green, yellow, orange decorative chalk**: Craf-T Products
- **page designer**: LeNae Gerig

Use chalks on white punched images to make your own look. Begin this page by chalking along side a ruler making six overlapping chalked lines. The square photos are double matted with a repeat of the chalked lines. The oval mat is simply chalked around the outside edge. The flowers were chalked before they were punched to make it easier and a heavy dot of chalk is in the center of each. Leaves were chalked after they were punched.

- **patterned Paper Pizazz**™: pink/orange dapple (*Great Backgrounds*)
- **solid Paper Pizazz**™: cream (*Soild Pastel Papers*)
- **1/2"-1" flower and leaf punches**: Family Treasures, Inc.
- **green, pink, yellow decorative chalks**: Craf-T Products
- **green pen**: Zig® Writer
- **page designer**: Amberly Beck

Use the empty space from a punched image as a stencil and chalk through it! The red and green color scheme comes from the tulips. Everything is double matted including the green swirls paper. The tulip silhouette punch was punched and the empty space (called negative space) was placed on a white square. Then chalk was used and the stencil removed. Another great use for punches and chalks!

- **patterned Paper Pizazz**™: green swirl (*Soft Tints*); ivy (*Floral Papers*); red tri-dot (*Dots, Checks, Plaids & Stripes*)
- **solid Paper Pizazz**™: white (*Plain Pastels*); red (*Plain Brights*)
- **tulip silhouette punch**: McGill, Inc.
- **red decorative chalk**: Craf-T Products
- **black pen**: Zig® Writer
- **page designer**: LeNae Gerig

Chalks can be used on black & white photos. With black & white photos you can use whatever colors you like. Using vellum for matting and the die-cut letters is a great choice to go with this rich collage paper. Using chalks to accent just certain parts of the photos keeps them from turning into full-color prints.

- **patterned Paper Pizazz™**: fleur-de-lis (*Collage Papers*); peach vellum (*Pastel Vellum Papers*)
- **solid Paper Pizazz™**: specialty gold (*Metallic Papers*, also by the sheet)
- **traveler letters**: Accu/Cut® Systems
- **red, yellow, orange, blue decorative chalks**: Craf-T Products
- **metallic gold pen**: Sakura Gelly Roll
- **page designer**: Shauna Berglund-Immel

Just the flowers and the hat are chalked in this photo. The pink and yellow chalk colors are carried out in the paper choices with extra chalking around the punched flowers and journaling circle.

- **patterned Paper Pizazz™**: pink and yellow floral, pink/yellow plaid (*Soft Tints*)
- **solid Paper Pizazz™**: pale yellow (*Plain Pastels*)
- **flower punch, ¼" circle punch**: McGill, Inc.
- **pink, yellow, blue decorative chalks**: Craf-T Products
- **black pen**: Zig® Writer
- **photography**: INVU Portraits
- **page designer**: Shauna Berglund-Immel

Little girls are precious gifts, wrapped in love serene. Their dresses tied with sashes and futures tied with dreams.
Kaelin, 1 year

Repeating an image from the photo is a good way to chalk. This popsicle with its blended colors wouldn't look the same if made from plain papers. Since chalks can be blended, the look is perfectly duplicated. With the colors are faded in the photo, bright blue and yellow summer colors do the trick!

- **patterned Paper Pizazz™**: blue stripe, blue dot (*Bright Tints*)
- **solid Paper Pizazz™**: ivory, cream, white (*Plain Pastels*); yellow (*Plain Brights*)
- **swirl punch**: Family Treasures, Inc.
- **ripple long scissors**: Fiskars®, Inc.
- **yellow, orange, red decorative chalks**: Craf-T Products
- **black pen**: Zig® Writer
- **page designer**: LeNae Gerig

Creative pen work and chalking are a dynamic duo! The pink pocket holds Kaelin's photo and a card. The horse is her favorite toy and appropriate on the pocket. Dark blue chalk is on the back legs and lightly around the edge and along the jaw of the horse. Pink is used on the heart, rocker, nose, tail and mane. Notice the wonderful flourish on the tail and mail and the pen work outlining the horse. Great stuff!

- **patterned Paper Pizazz™**: baby pattern (*Annie Lang's Heartwarming Papers*); pink stripes, pink swirls (*Soft Tints*)
- **solid Paper Pizazz™**: white, light blue (*Plain Pastels*)
- **baby Punch-Out™**: *Annie's Kids Punch-Outs™*
- **rocking horse die-cut**: Accu/Cut® Systems
- **scallop scissors**: Fiskars®, Inc.
- **blue, pink decorative chalks**: Craf-T Products
- **black pen**: Zig® Writer
- **page designer**: Shauna Berglund-Immel

© &™ Accu/Cut® Systems

Laser lace can be chalked to match your page. Use a cotton swab to apply chalk to the lace. Cut along the curved edge of the lace with straight scissors. Place the lace over the edge of the matted photo and mat them together with light peach paper. A bit of the chalked lace is a lovely touch around the journaling oval.

- **patterned Paper Pizazz™**: gray and peach swirl, 1929 (*Black & White Photos*); peach moiré (*Pretty Papers,* also by the sheet); laser lace (*Romantic Papers,* also by the sheet)
- **solid Paper Pizazz™**: peach, ivory, gray (*Solid Muted*); white (*Plain Pastels*)
- **mini antique Victorian scissors**: Family Treasures, Inc.
- **peach decorative chalk**: Craf-T Products
- **page designer**: LeNae Gerig

Use chalk to add color to patterned paper. This patterned paper has a lovely blend of whites and creams but for this photo a touch of peach is perfect. Susan chalked along the base of the rose petals and a bit of green chalk to the base of the leaves. Peach vellum is ideal for the matting to carry the color. Because gold metallic is actually on the patterned paper, a gold mat, gold journaling and gold photo corners are a nice tie in. A peach shoestring bow is the final touch.

- **patterned Paper Pizazz™**: roses (*Bj's Handpainted & Gold Papers*); peach vellum (*Pastel Vellum Papers*)
- **solid Paper Pizazz™**: specialty gold (*Metallic Papers,* also by the sheet)
- **gold photo corners**: Canson-Talens, Inc.
- **green, peach decorative chalks**: Craf-T Products
- **9" length of 1¹/₂" wide sheer peach ribbon**: C.M. Offray &, Son, Inc.
- **metallic gold pen**: Sakura Gelly Roll
- **page designer**: Susan Cobb

Chalks make very realistic die-cuts. Gary's shirt sets the stage for this western page. Although they look real, the buttons are punched circles with a pen outline, four black dots and a gray chalked center. The die-cut boot is cut from three papers and layered as shown. Black chalk outlines the boot with white chalk used for the loop design. Pen work adds the final details.

- **patterned Paper Pizazz™**: denim (*Country*, also by the sheet); red tartan (*Christmas*, also by the sheet); elephant skin (*Wild Things*); black leather, brown brush strokes (*Textured Papers*)
- **solid Paper Pizazz™**: white (*Plain Pastels*)
- **boot die-cut**: Accu/Cut® Systems
- **¹/₂" circle punch**: Marvy® Uchida
- **deckle scissors**: Family Treasures, Inc.
- **black, gray, white decorating chalk**: Craf-T Products
- **white pen**: Pentel Gel Roller
- **black pen**: Marvy® Uchida Medallion
- **foam mounting tape**: Scotch® Brand
- **page designer**: Shauna Berglund-Immel

© & ® Accu/Cut® Systems

Chalking used inside cut shapes adds another, yet subtle look. What a fun collection of stripped and dotted papers all taking their cue from the sweet moon and star paper. Since the photo is black & white, Susan lightly chalked blue on the baby's shirt. Pink chalk is gently spread along the mat but close to the white mat and on the star but only in the center. The little moon is cut from the paper under the photo and added to the star. What fun pen work throughout this page!

- **patterned Paper Pizazz™**: yellow stripe, yellow dots (*Soft Tints*); moon and stars (*Annie Lang's Heartwarming Papers*)
- **solid Paper Pizazz™**: white (*Plain Pastel*); black (*Solid Jewel Tones*)
- **star die-cut**: Accu/Cut® Systems
- **yellow, gold, pink decorating chalks**: Craf-T Products
- **black pens**: Zig® Millenium and Zig® Writer
- **page designer**: Susan Cobb

© &™ Accu/Cut® Systems

Fold

Terrific Paper Techniques

O kay, we admit it—we LOVE paper! We love designing it, selecting it and especially, we love using it. This chapter focuses on eight paper techniques. We'll begin with simple snipping. That is, cutting apart an all-over patterned paper. It's especially effective with papers showing food, yum! See pages 76-81 for some terrific ideas.

Have you tried using double-sided foam tape? It is about $1/16$" thick and can lift things off the album page. Not a big lift, just a little bit that provides a wonderful look. You'll find eight sample album pages to get you started. Bet you'll find a lot of ways to use foam tape (or foam dots) once you get started!

Collage looks are everywhere, on cards, wrapping paper and now in scrapbooking papers. It's a look that may require some practice, but for the right photos and with the right collection of papers, it's a fun technique. Come on, give it a try.

You've probably seen mosaics using tiles shown in home decorating magazines. Let's bridge the gap and try it in scrapbooks. You can do all-over mosaics or just highlight a border. We have samples for you!

Probably the opposite of exact-cutting mosaics is free-hand torn paper. Here are samples of torn paper piecing, torn scenes as well as torn strips and borders. One note: Be sure to use printed paper (even if it is plain colored) so when you tear, you'll get a white edge.

Tea bag folding and paper quilting have become incredibly popular with scrapbookers. Making three simple folded shapes (a kite, diamond and square) can produce the most stunning results. You can use especially designed tea bag folding squares or make your own using patterned. Here are suggestions using specific patterned papers. The key to amazing paper quilting is having the geometric shapes figured out. We've done the math for you and here are samples to get you started.

Finally, here's some fancy knife work. These scrapbook specialists have done amazing things with a little snip here and a slice there. Take a look for yourself.

PATTERNED PAPER TECHNIQUES

Using all over patterned paper to create some new pizazz!

Doesn't the cut popcorn paper add a great look to this page? Amy cut around popcorn kernels using an X-acto® knife to get into the nooks and crannies. She piled them on the bottom of the page and into a popcorn bag die cut. The matching photo mat draws the eye upward, and the film strip journaling plaque plays right into the theme.

- **patterned Paper Pizazz™**: filmstrips (*Vacation*); red and white stripe (*Ho Ho Ho,* also by the sheet); popcorn (*Yummy Papers,* also by the sheet)
- **solid Paper Pizazz™**: yellow (*Plain Brights*); black (*Solid Jewel Tones*); white (*Plain Pastels*)
- **popcorn container die cut**: Accu/Cut® Systems
- **X-acto knife®** and cutting surface
- **1/2" long rectangle punch**: McGill, Inc.
- **page designer**: Amy Gustafson

Every Friday night at our house is movie night! Daddy makes popcorn, and we all decide on a movie, turn off all the lights, and pile on the couch!

Two patterned papers are cut apart to make this travel page with style and flair. A stamp pattern-edged scissors was used to trim around groups of stamps, while straight scissors are perfect on the letters paper. Plain black mats are all the photos need. And, oui, the Eiffel Tower die cut is very Français!

- **patterned Paper Pizazz™**: letters, red moiré (*Black & White Photos,* also by the sheet); stamps (*Vacation #2,* also by the sheet)
- **solid Paper Pizazz™**: black (*Solid Jewel Tones*)
- **Eiffel Tower die cut**: Accu/Cut® Systems
- **stamp scissors**: Fiskars®, Inc.
- **white pen**: Pentel Milky Gel Roller
- **page designer**: LeNae Gerig

© & ™ Accu/Cut® Systems

Frosted leaves plus fern vellum plus burgundy crushed suede plus plaid all add up to one great page. That's because all the colors come from the same family, and the most distinctive patterns—the leaves and the plaid—are separated by subtle patterns. Trimming around the frosted leaves adds an interesting edge, and Susan chalked some of the vellum fern leaves for a bit of color.

- **patterned Paper Pizazz™**: brown plaid, frosted leaves (*The Great Outdoors*); vellum with ferns (*Vellum Papers*, also by the sheet); burgundy suede (*For Black & White Photos*, also by the sheet)
- **solid Paper Pizazz™**: mauve, peach (*Solid Muted Colors*); black (*Solid Jewel Tones*)
- **maple leaf die cut**: Ellison® Craft & Design
- **peach, pink decorating chalks**: Craf-T Products
- **mauve pen**: Marvy® Uchida
- **metallic gold pen**: Zebra® Jimnie® Gel Rollerball
- **page designer**: Susan Cobb

© & ™ Ellison® Craft & Design

Here's an excellent example of building upon the theme established in the photos. Shauna trimmed around individual leaves and "piled" them up to echo the leaf pile Spencer is playing in. Some are adhered with foam dots for an even more dimensional effect. The plaid background paper echoes the colors of the leaves. The feel is bright, vibrant and playful.

- **patterned Paper Pizazz™**: 2 sheets fall leaves (*Holidays & Seasons*, also by the sheet); gold/brown/rust plaid (by the sheet)
- **solid Paper Pizazz™**: yellow (*Solid Muted Colors*); red (*Solid Jewel Tones*)
- **X-acto® knife and cutting surface**
- **foam Pop Dots**: All Night Media®, Inc.
- **black pen**: Zig® Writer
- **page designer**: Shauna Berglund-Immel

Motifs cut from your background paper make instantly coordinated page embellishments. After Susan cut the rose paper on this page into a 10½" square, she trimmed three yellow roses from the leftovers and matted them on pale yellow. Adhered to the page with foam tape, they bridge the photos and both patterned papers. Very pretty!

- **patterned Paper Pizazz**™: yellow stripe, yellow roses (*Soft Florals & Patterns*)
- **solid Paper Pizazz**™: pale yellow, ivory (*Plain Pastels*)
- **small heart die cut**: Accu/Cut® Systems
- **metallic gold pen**: Zebra® Jimnie® Gel Rollerball
- **foam mounting tape**: Scotch® Brand
- **page designer**: Susan Cobb

© & ™ Accu/Cut® Systems

A bouquet and garland of creamy white lilies patterned paper frame the photos on this page and echo the bride's flowers. Susan outlined the lilies with gold (before gluing them onto the page) to separate them from the background paper and repeat the narrow gold photo mats. The subtle patterned background paper provides a soft setting for this important day. The bow is a lovely finishing touch—and don't worry, ribbon is acid-free.

- **patterned Paper Pizazz**™: butterfly lace (*"Lace" Papers*); lilies (*Soft Florals & Patterns*)
- **solid Paper Pizazz**™: pale yellow (*Solid Pastel Papers*); specialty gold (*Metallic Papers*, also by the sheet)
- **heart template**: Extra Special Products Corp.
- **15"of 1½" wide ivory ribbon**: Wrights®
- **X-acto® knife and cutting surface**
- **metallic gold pen**: Zebra® Jimnie® Gel Rollerball
- **page designer**: Shauna Berglund-Immel

These photos look like they're sitting in a basket of jellybeans! To achieve this effect, Susan first matted two photos and silhouetted one, then placed them on the page and lightly marked where she wanted jelly beans to overlap them. She used an X-acto® knife to trim around those jelly beans and tucked the photos underneath. This fancy knifework technique works with any three-dimensional all-over patterned paper.

- **patterned Paper Pizazz**™: jelly beans (*Yummy Papers*)
- **solid Paper Pizazz**™: yellow, green (*Plain Brights*)
- **green pen**: Zig® Writer
- **X-acto® knife and cutting surface**
- **page designer**: Susan Cobb

The knifework technique used on this page is similar to the jellybean page, but a pale blue vellum photo mat makes a pond for Spencer's fishing. To add dimension, Shauna trimmed a few stones from the background paper (she used the paper under the photo to avoid cutting into another sheet) and adhered them at the vellum edges with foam tape.

- **patterned Paper Pizazz**™: beach pebbles (by the sheet)
- **solid Paper Pizazz**™: white (*Plain Pastels*); sky blue vellum (*Pastel Vellum Papers*)
- **font**: Cockadoodle Design Page Doodlers CD-ROM
- **photographer**: INVU Photography
- **foam mounting tape**: Scotch® Brand
- **page designer**: Shauna Berglund-Immel

"Strawberry Fields Forever"
Kaitlyn Llorens
Hillsboro, Oregon
June 2000

A pail of plump strawberries is a delicious complement to this page. Using the patterns on page 141, cut a pail from strawberries paper, a rim from white and a handle from silver. Draw linework on the rim and glue it to the strawberries paper shape. Place beneath patterned vellum, trace the pail shape, cut out the vellum pail and glue it to the strawberries pail. Mat the bucket and handle on black and glue on the handle. Cut out individual strawberries and glue into the bucket and onto the page as shown, adhering with foam tape.

- **patterned Paper Pizazz™**: yellow roses with border (*Janie Dawson's Special Companions*); strawberries (*Yummy Papers*); yellow vellum with heart bouquets (*Colored Vellum Papers*)
- **solid Paper Pizazz™**: white (*Plain Pastels*); black (*Solid Jewel Tones*); specialty silver (*Pearlescent Papers*, also by the sheet)
- **foam Pop Dots**: All Night Media®, Inc.
- **X-acto® knife and cutting surface**
- **mini scallop scissors**: Fiskars®, Inc.
- **page designer**: Shauna Berglund-Immel

We loved Joanne's fun photos, her clever journaling and her innovative use of ¼" paper ties around the mat on Fletcher's photo. And yes, Joanne did make Fletcher's costume. She tells us, "I design and make his costumes. He's been Sherlock Holmes, a prince, an Indian and a cow. I am very proud of Fletcher. He is a therapy dog and visits hospitals and nursing homes." This third place winner in our Autumn Pages with Pizazz™ contest is a beauty!

- **patterned Paper Pizazz™**: fall leaves (*Holidays & Seasons*, also by the sheet)
- **solid Paper Pizazz™**: yellow, orange (*Solid Muted Colors*); white (*Plain Pastels*); hunter green (*Solid Jewel Tones*); dark green (*Perfect Pairs™ 12"x12" Green & Burgundy*)
- **solid cardstock**: brick red
- **leaf punch**: Family Treasures, Inc.
- **large metallic gold letter stickers**: Stamp Cabana
- **small metallic gold letter stickers**: Provo Craft®
- **page designer**: Joanne Lee

3-D LOOKS

Techniques to add a whole new dimension to your pages!

With just a twist of paper you'll get a pretty border. Just cut ¾" wide strips of patterned paper and twist each twice at approximately 1½" intervals. Because twisting shortens the strips, glue them to the page after twisting, then trim the ends even. Thin yellow stripes give the border more oomph, and a four-layer mat really makes the photo of adorable Samantha pop off the page.

- **patterned Paper Pizazz™**: lady bugs and bees (also by the sheet); black with white dots (*Black & White Coordinating Colors™*)
- **solid Paper Pizazz™**: white (*Plain Pastels*); yellow (*Plain Brights*); black (*Solid Jewel Tones*)
- **deckle scissors**: Family Treasures, Inc.
- **white pen**: Pentel Milky Gel Roller
- **page designer**: LeNae Gerig

Fancy knifework creates a special effect for a very special photo. Shauna cut the white spaces from lattice background paper and layered it over roses paper to resemble flowers climbing a garden gate. A few of the same roses overlap the photo to draw the eye and unite the page elements. The pink flowers and balloons in the photo inspired Shauna's color choices. You could also make your own lattice from plain white paper.

- **patterned Paper Pizazz™**: pink and white roses (*Blooming Blossoms*); lattice (*Our Wedding*); pink satin (*Very Pretty Papers*, also by the sheet)
- **solid Paper Pizazz™**: white (*Plain Pastels*); hunter green (*Solid Muted Colors*)
- **pink and green pens**: Zig® Writer
- **X-acto® knife and cutting surface**
- **foam Pop Dots**: All Night Media®, Inc.
- **page designer**: Shauna Berglund-Immel

Using a background paper with a beautiful pre-printed border like this one means you can create a gorgeous page in a snap! Daisies cut from a coordinating sheet and three vellum butterflies are adhered to the photo corners to echo the border. The clever journaling—it's part of the butterfly's trail—adds a touch of whimsy. Foam tape is under the butterflies' bodies to leave their wings free.

- **patterned Paper Pizazz**™: green with flowers and butterflies border, flowers and butterflies (*Vintage Papers*); vellum with butterflies (*Painted Vellum*)
- **solid Paper Pizazz**™: blue (*Plain Brights*); specialty gold (*Metallic Papers*, also by the sheet)
- **black pen**: Zig® Writer
- metallic **gold pen**: Pentel Gel Roller
- **foam dots**: All Night Media®, Inc. Pop Dots
- **X-acto® knife and cutting surface**
- **foam mounting tape**: Scotch® Brand
- **page designer**: Shauna Berglund-Immel

This page delivers a surprise—frogs and daisies and bugs that hop right off the page! Debbie chose images from the border at the page bottom, cut identical motifs from a duplicate border paper, and used foam tape to adhere them directly on top of the image. This technique, combined with the heart buttons, adds a fun 3-D effect to the page.

- **patterned Paper Pizazz**™: bugs and snails, 2 sheets turtles and frogs (*Annie Lang's Cheerful & Charming Papers*)
- **solid Paper Pizazz**™: ivory (*Plain Pastels*); purple (*Solid Jewel Tones*); muted green (*Solid Muted Colors*)
- **frog and daisy Punch-Out**™: *Annie Lang's Cheerful & Charming Punch-Outs*™
- **1" wavy square punch, Victorian corner punch**: Family Treasures, Inc.
- **¾" wide wood heart buttons**: "Dress It Up" A Jesse James Co.
- **12" length of light green embroidery floss**
- **foam mounting tape**: Scotch® Brand
- **page designer**: Debbie Peterson

Borders adhered with foam tape define the edges of this page, directing the eye to the photos in the center. These borders were cut from patterned paper, matted and punched for extra decoration. Brass o-rings connect the letters of the girls' names so they dangle like beads on a necklace. Debbie tinted the edges of the white journaling plaque using a stamp pad and a cosmetic sponge.

- **patterned Paper Pizazz™**: mauve tiles (*Pretty & Classy Papers*)
- **solid Paper Pizazz™**: burgundy (*Solid Jewel Tones*); white (*Plain Pastels*)
- **1/16" hole and Victorian corner slot punches**: Family Treasures, Inc.
- **5/8" circle and 3/4" wide bow punches**: McGill, Inc.
- **corner punch**: Family Treasures, Inc.
- **5/8" and 7/8" butterfly punches**: Family Treasures
- **letter stickers**: Provo Craft®
- **deckle scissors**: Family Treasures, Inc.
- **brass o-rings** (adjust the number according to how many letters are in the name)
- **burgundy stamp pad**
- **cosmetic sponge**
- **burgundy pen**: Zig® Writer
- **foam mounting tape**: Scotch® Brand
- **page designer**: Debbie Peterson

The lovely paper collage flower border on this page beautifully frames the photo while echoing the garland behind the bride and groom. Shauna started with a sheet of hydrangea-bordered vellum centered on lattice background paper. She chose floral printed papers, cut individual blossoms and arranged them on and around the vellum. The top layer and the butterflies are all attached with foam tape. Journaling plaques are tucked among the flowers for a lovely Victorian look.

- **patterned Paper Pizazz™**: hydrangeas (*Pretty Papers*, also by the sheet); lattice (*Our Wedding Day*); white flowers, purple flowers, pink roses (*Floral Papers*); vellum with hydrangea border (*Floral Vellum Papers*)
- **solid Paper Pizazz™**: specialty silver (*Pearlescent Papers*, also by the sheet); white (*Plain Pastels*)
- **vellum butterfly Cut-Outs™**: *Vellum Cut-Outs™*
- **Victorian scissors**: Fiskars®, Inc.
- **X-acto® knife and cutting surface**
- **metallic silver pen**: Marvy® Uchida
- **black pen**: Marvy® Uchida
- **foam mounting tape**: Scotch® Brand
- **page designer**: Shauna Berglund-Immel

A little 3-D foam tape photo manipulation yields big results on this page! LeNae color copied each photo, then silhouette cut the car and Molly. She used foam tape to adhere the silhouettes to the original photos. The dimensional effect makes Grandpa's two "American Beauties" stand out and emphasizes the connection between them. The red roses on the right are cut from the roses paper and also attached with foam tape

- **patterned Paper Pizazz™**: navy blue suede, red roses (*Heritage Papers*, also by the sheet)
- **solid Paper Pizazz™**: specialty gold (*Metallic Papers*, also by the sheet); white (*Plain Pastels*)
- **dots and lines border Punch-Out™**: *Heritage Punch-Outs™*
- **metallic gold calligraphy pen**: Sakura of America
- **foam mounting tape**: Scotch® Brand
- **page designer**: LeNae Gerig

Two special photo effects combine to put extra emphasis on the subject—little Zoë splashing in the puddles. Shauna color-copied the photo (color copies are best even for black & white photos) and used a red pencil to color Zoë's coat. She silhouette cut Zoë and used foam tape to adhere the silhouette to the original photo. A thin red photo mat and the die cut bring out Zoë's raincoat.

- **patterned Paper Pizazz™**: raindrops (*Child's Play*, also by the sheet)
- **solid Paper Pizazz™**: red, blue (*Plain Brights*); white (*Plain Pastels*)
- **umbrella die cut**: Accu/Cut® Systems
- **red pencil**: EK Success Ltd.
- **white pen**: Pentel of America, Ltd.
- **blue pen**: Zebra® Jimnie® Gel Rollerball
- **foam mounting tape**: Scotch® Brand
- **page designer**: Shauna Berglund-Immel

© & ™ Accu/Cut® Systems

Use foam tape or dots to lift the smaller oval photos and overlap them on the larger ones—this adds texture and interest as well as saving space. Foam was also used to lift the larger lower photos and to layer the flower and leaf punches for a 3-D effect. To echo the Mickey Mouse silhouettes on the background papers, each flower center is a Mickey head formed from round punches.

Growing Family Ties!
Washington & Iowa Peterson's at Disneyland Park.
1999
We met in California for Cami's wedding and decided to spend some family bonding time!

Disney characters ©Disney Enterprises, Inc.
Used by permission from Disney Enterprises, Inc.

- **patterned Paper Pizazz™**: blue stripes with Mickey outline, red/blue plaid with Mickey silhouettes (*Mickey Mouse Simple Backgrounds*)
- **solid Paper Pizazz™**: red, dark green (*Solid Jewel Tones*); medium blue (*Solid Muted Colors*)
- **Little Letter stickers**: Making Memories™
- **Mickey punch**: All Night Media®, Inc.
- **1" wide flower, ⅝" long leaf punches**: Family Treasures, Inc.
- **deckle scissors**: Family Treasures, Inc.
- **Coluzzle oval cutter**: Provo Craft®
- **page designer**: Debbie Peterson

The center page turns to offer a whole new spread in this clever design (we've outlined the smaller center page in green to make it more visible—there's not really a green border!). Notice how each side of the inner page uses a different Mickey paper to coordinate with the outer pages.

For a neater look, the top of the center page protector was cut off even with the page top. The two remaining holes are enough to secure the page in the album.

Disney characters ©Disney Enterprises, Inc.
Used by permission from Disney Enterprises, Inc.

Disney characters ©Disney Enterprises, Inc.
Used by permission from Disney Enterprises, Inc.

- **patterned Paper Pizazz™**: Mickey beach stripes, black with red Mickey Silhouettes (*Mickey Mouse Simple Backgrounds*)
- **solid Paper Pizazz™**: red (*Plain Brights*); black (*Solid Jewel Tones*); white (*Plain Pastels*)
- **white letter stickers**: Provo Craft®
- **deckle scissors**: Family Treasures , Inc.
- **Coluzzle circle and oval cutters**: Provo Craft®
- **white pen**: Pentel
- **black pen**: Zig® Writer
- **page designer**: Amberly Beck

COLLAGE TECHNIQUES

Ideas for collages that turn your pages into works of art!

The little treasures gathered on your journeys are as much a part of your experience as the photos. Here, a layered collage of several papers—all with similar textured or landscape themes—sets the stage for a photo of grandma beachcombing and a few of her findings. Use foam tape to secure heavy items such as shells to your pages. Because it includes things grandma thought pretty enough to pick up, this page tells a more complete story than if it only showed a photo. You could also color copy the treasures and glue that in place.

- **patterned Paper Pizazz™**: burlap (*Country*, also by the sheet); beach pebbles (by the sheet); map (*Military Papers*); gold crackled (*Spattered, Crackled, Sponged*)
- **solid Paper Pizazz™**: black (*Solid Jewel Tones*); mauve (*Solid Muted Colors*)
- **volcano scissors**: Fiskars®, Inc
- **4" of 3-ply jute**
- **three 3/4" wide seashell pieces**
- **Black pen**: Zig® Writer
- **foam mounting tage**: Scotch® Brand
- **page designer**: LeNae Gerig

This collage layout conveys the activity and excitement of Amy's whirlwind trip around France. A luggage tag created from the pattern provided and embroidery floss, is the perfect journaling plaque. Because the layered and patterned papers make a vibrant background, the photos are matted simply with straight edges. The cobblestone paper is a perfect European background. This page, showcasing a photo from each of Amy's destinations, would make an excellent introduction to her vacation album.

- **patterned Paper Pizazz™**: cobblestones (by the sheet); stamps, travel stickers (*Vacation #2*, also by the sheet); burlap (*Textured Papers*, also by the sheet); letters (*Black & White Photos*, also by the sheet)
- **solid Paper Pizazz™**: pale yellow, white, ivory (*Plain Pastels*); brown (*Solid Muted Colors*); black (*Solid Jewel Tones*)
- **1/4" hole punch**: McGill, Inc.
- **9" of ivory embroidery floss**
- **page designer**: Amy Gustafson

Vellum is a great addition to most collage pages and it's certainly a surprise in this military page. Yet it works! Cut the map paper in half diagonally as shown and mount it over camouflage paper. Cut small pieces of green and brown paper from a corner of camouflage paper and use to make diamonds. Glue one over other and outline with black pen.

- **patterned Paper Pizazz™**: vellum dots (*Vellum Papers*, also by the sheet) camouflage, gear, map (*Military Papers*)
- **solid Paper Pizazz™**: black (*Solid Jewel Tones*); white (*Plain Pastels*)
- **deckle scissors**: Family Treasures, Inc.
- **white pen**: Pentel Milky Gel Roller
- **black pen**: Zig® Writer
- **page designer**: LeNae Gerig

The collage background page comes ready-to-use as a printed patterned paper. Yet, a simple layered collage of colored and white-on white vellums is a perfect accent. Notice several of the vellums and the leaf are edged with a silver pen. Pretty! The leaf pattern is on page 77.

- **patterned Paper Pizazz™**: blue/green collage *Collage Papers*); blue dot vellum, purple hollow dot vellum (*Colored Vellum Papers*); vellum with ferns (*Vellum Papers*, also by the sheet)
- **solid Paper Pizazz™**: green vellum (*Pastel Vellum Papers*); specialty silver (*Pearlescent Papers*); lavender (*Solid Muted Colors*)
- **maple leaf die cut**: Ellison® Craft & Design
- **metallic silver pen**: Pentel Gel Roller
- **page designer**: Susan Cobb

This page looks like a trick-or-treater's dream! Amy created it by cutting elements from several candy-patterned papers and arranging them on a background of chocolate chips. (Yum!) The candies overlapping the photos make them look so real you could reach into the page and grab a handful! Bright yellow mats keep the photos and journaling in focus.

- **patterned Paper Pizazz™**: colorful candies, jelly beans, chocolate chips, candy corn (*Yummy Papers*, jelly beans, chocolate chips and candy corn are also available by the sheet)
- **solid Paper Pizazz™**: yellow (*Plain Brights*); white (*Plain Pastels*)
- **black pen**: Marvy® Artist
- **page designer**: Amy Gustafson

School's in and it's time for friends, football games, fun outings—and teen-themed scrapbook pages. This collage layout, resembling a bulletin board covered with photos and tickets, is colorful and vibrant—just like a teenager's life. The bright hearts, coils and stars paper and tie-dye paper work on the same page because they're separated by the more muted bulletin board and denim papers. Of course, the photos are double matted so they stand out. The tickets come from another patterned paper.

- **patterned Paper Pizazz™**: jeans, tie-dye, tickets (*Teen Years*; jeans and tie-dye also by the sheet); bulletin board (*School Days*); hearts, coils and stars (by the sheet)
- **solid Paper Pizazz™**: yellow (*Plain Brights*); blue (*Teen Years*)
- **tack Cut-Outs™**: *Paper Pizazz™ School Days*
- **black pen**: Zig® Writer
- **page designer**: Emily Gustafson

Arranged into a collage, odd and duplicate photos of Molly get a scrapbook page all their own. Shauna arranged and glued them on plain paper and added a vellum overlay to create a soft focus that imparts an air of nostalgia. A few precious baby photos rest on top of the vellum and the "Through the Years" journaling ties the whole page together. A collage like this one is a great use for extra photos that don't seem to fit elsewhere in your album. What a treasure!

- **solid Paper Pizazz™**: tan vellum (*Pastel Vellum Papers*); light blue, white (*Plain Pastels*)
- **stamp scissors**: Fiskars®, Inc.
- **blue glitter pen**: Sakura Gelly Roll
- **black pen**: Marvy® Artist
- **page designer**: Shauna Berglund-Immel

Overlapping papers in soft tones make a lovely collage for special wedding photos. The pastel vellums allow the pattern beneath to peek through, adding another dimension to the design.

- **patterned Paper Pizazz™**: hydrangeas, iris, purple stripe (*Soft Florals & Patterns*)
- **solid Paper Pizazz™**: blue lavender vellum, lavender vellum, plum pink vellum (*Pastel Vellum Papers*); specialty silver (*Pearlescent Papers*, also by the sheet); ivory (*Plain Pastels*)
- **purple pen**: Marvy® Uchida Medallion Drawing Pen
- **metallic silver pen**: Pentel Gel Roller
- **page designer**: Susan Cobb

MAKING MOSAIC PAGES

Creative cropping becomes a marvelous mosaic!

When you have a photo with a well-defined subject on a pretty background, try the creative and interesting mosaic technique shown on this page. Cut the photo into sections, making sure the subject is in the largest piece. Mat the pieces, then arrange them slightly apart and offset on a background sheet. Thin border strips mimic the spaces between the photo pieces, and decorative trim on the page sides echoes the angular photo shapes.

- **patterned Paper Pizazz™**: blue handmade (*Light Great Backgrounds*)
- **solid Paper Pizazz™**: hunter green, black (*Solid Jewel Tones*); white (*Plain Pastels*)
- **⅝" and ⅞" wide butterfly punches**: Family Treasures, Inc.
- **letter stickers**: Provo Craft®
- **peaks scissors**: Fiskars®, Inc.
- **page designer**: Debbie Peterson

These photos were cut into mosaics using a technique similar to the "Meg" page (above), but Debbie chose rectangles instead of triangles. Matting the pieces on white, then green, gives the effect of looking out a window at a little boy playing in the yard. To make the leaf border, cut a 1" wide white strip, punch leaf shapes from it and mat on dark green. The plaid background paper is the perfect choice!

- **patterned Paper Pizazz™**: green/yellow plaid (*Jewel Plaids*)
- **solid Paper Pizazz™**: hunter green (*Solid Jewel Tones*); white (*Plain Pastels*)
- **½" wide and ⅞" wide maple leaf punches**: Marvy® Uchida
- **⅜" and ⅞" wide oak leaf punches**: Family Treasures, Inc.
- **letter stickers**: Provo Craft®
- **page designer**: Debbie Peterson

The first place winner in our Autumn Pages with Pizazz™ contest is Jackie Phelps. She combined photos and patterned paper into a page-sized mosaic with a classic feel. She printed the journaling onto patterned paper, then cut the paper and photos into 1⅛" squares. (Hint: The hardest part of making a mosaic page is keeping the pieces in order!) Arrange the paper and photo squares on a solid sheet with a uniform 1/16"-1/8" space between them. Mat the sheet onto matching patterned paper to make a page-framing border. This page is certainly terrific!

- **patterned Paper Pizazz™**: ivy on cream (*A Woman's Scrapbook*, also by the sheet)
- **solid Paper Pizazz™**: sage green, orange (*Solid Muted Colors*)
- **ripple scissors**: Fiskars®, Inc.
- **page designer**: Jackie Phelps

Both photos were enlarged and cut along with the sand patterned paper into 1" squares. (Shauna made sure not to cut the photo across the Ali's or Gideon's face.) Reassemble them on a background sheet with a little separation between them. Notice that the top photo is divided by sand squares—a little decorative touch.

- **patterned Paper Pizazz™**: sand (*Textured Papers*); crushed suede (*Black & White Photos*, also by the sheet)
- **black pen**: Marvy® Artist
- **page designer**: Shauna Berglund-Immel

This mosaic page was quick to pull together—yet the results are classy and elegant. Susan chose two colors from the sponged background paper, then cut 1" squares for the border and ½" squares for the photo mat. Slightly tilting the photo keeps things from looking too orderly, and silver penwork details add the finishing touch.

- **patterned Paper Pizazz**™: purple sponged (*Pretty Papers*, also by the sheet)
- **solid Paper Pizazz**™: light aqua (*Plain Pastels*); purple (*Solid Jewel Tones*)
- **metallic silver pen**: Pentel Milky Gel Roller
- **page designer**: Susan Cobb

The colors and patterns in this mosaic make it look as though it could have been discovered in an ancient Roman villa. Shauna used a square punch to make quick work of the ⅜" squares in the page border and center, and cut 1" squares for the blue border. Anywhere there was an odd space to fill, she just cut a square to fit. An orange background gives this page a playful appeal; use blue or green for a more understated look. Again, the tilted photo keeps the page interesting.

- **patterned Paper Pizazz**™: orange, blue and green bubbles; blue tiles (*Bright Great Backgrounds*)
- **solid Paper Pizazz**™: orange, blue green (*Plain Brights*)
- **½" square punch**: Family Treasures, Inc.
- **green pen**: Pentel Milky Gel Roller
- **page designer**: Shauna Berglund-Immel

Waves made of various blue patterned papers wash around the edges of a sandy beach on this stunning mosaic page. To recreate it, cut your five papers (four blue and one sand) into roughly ⅜" squares (uneven edges are okay—they add to the handmade effect). You'll need about 200 squares for the waves and 250 for the sand. Arrange them on a solid background, cutting some squares into triangles where needed.

- **patterned Paper Pizazz™**: raindrops (*Child's Play*, also by the sheet); pool water, sand (*Vacation #2*, pool water also by the sheet); blue checks and swirls (*A Girl's Scrapbook*, also by the sheet); navy tiles (by the sheet)
- **solid Paper Pizazz™**: tan (*Plain Pastels*); light blue (*Plain Brights*)
- **X-acto® knife and cutting surface**
- **metal-edged ruler**
- **brown pen**: Zig® Writer
- **page designer**: Amy Gustafson

Rings of color and pattern in this mosaic page border draw the eye inward toward the photo. Papers printed with similar patterns were cut into 1" squares and arranged on a background sheet with just a bit of the solid color showing between the squares. Notice the outer mosaic row is a different pattern and the inner row is a third pattern. This layout incorporates four color families—that's a lot—but it's effective because all the colors have the same intensity. It adds up to a fun, bright look.

- **patterned Paper Pizazz™**: green plaid, blue plaid, red/yellow plaid, yellow swirls, yellow dots (*Bright Tints*)
- **solid Paper Pizazz™**: white (*Solid Pastel Papers*)
- **fish die-cut**: Accu/Cut® Systems
- **black pen**: Marvy® Artist
- **page designer**: Shauna Berglund-Immel

TORN PAPER

No scissors needed for these interesting looks! Scrapbookers are tearing paper to create stylish paper piecing, mats, borders—all kinds of things. The following pages will give you some great ideas for using torn paper.

This page was almost entirely scissors-free! Use an X-acto® knife to cut slits in the edges of the background sheet, then weave torn ¾" plaid strips through them. Tear solid and patterned mats for each photo. How to tear such straight edges? Just hold a ruler firmly on the paper and pull the paper to tear along the ruler's edge. Tearing printed papers will give you that nice, white edge.

- **patterned Paper Pizazz™**: Peach dots and peach plaid (*Making Heritage Scrapbook Pages*)
- **solid Paper Pizazz™**: Tan (*Solid Muted Colors*)
- **X-acto® knife and cutting surface**
- **metal-edged ruler**
- **tan Photo Twins™ photo tinting pen**: EK Success Ltd.
- **black pen**: Zig® Writer
- **page designer**: LeNae Gerig

Torn paper is useful for creating the look of, well … torn paper. Use the patterns (the tag pattern is on page 86 and the box pattern is on page 141). Tear along just the top edges of the gift box, then fold the box where indicated by the dashed line. Letting this photo of Daniel emerge from an opened gift box is a great example of developing the theme of the photo! It would also be perfect for a birthday page.

- **patterned Paper Pizazz™**: green with stars (*Dots, Checks, Plaids & Stripes*, also by the sheet); Christmas Plaid (*Ho Ho Ho*, also by the sheet)
- **solid Paper Pizazz™**: red (*Plain Brights*); specialty gold (*Metallic Papers*, also by the sheet)
- **confetti die cut**: Accu/Cut® Systems
- **black pen, calligraphy pen**: Zig® Writer
- **page designer**: Amy Gustafson

Rough torn paper edges are just right for creating scenes of sand dunes and ocean waves. LeNae created this scene by layering blue paper over oatmeal and brown papers. To get a white edge on your torn paper, as shown here, place the paper on your work surface face up. Grab the farthest edge of the sheet and pull it toward yourself. (This only works with a white-backed paper such as Paper Pizazz™.)

- **patterned Paper Pizazz™**: clouds (*Vacation*, also by the sheet); green swirl (*Pretty Papers*, also by the sheet)
- **solid Paper Pizazz™**: dark blue, tan, oatmeal (*Solid Muted Colors*)
- **⅝" long foot punch**: Marvy® Uchida
- **black pen**: Zig® Writer
- **page designer**: LeNae Gerig

SeaSide July 2000

To create the fluffy, bumpy texture of a snowman, tear him from paper. Tear 2" and 3" white circles for the head and body. Transfer the carrot, hat, scarf, arms and broom patterns to solid or patterned papers and cut them out. Mat each shape (except the arms) on black and glue onto the snowman. Tuck him into torn snowdrifts along with a silhouetted photo.

- **patterned Paper Pizazz™**: snow people, red with white dots, white with red and green dots, green plaid (*Ho Ho Ho*, also by the sheet)
- **solid Paper Pizazz™**: green, orange, black (*Solid Jewel Tones*); brown (*Solid Muted Colors*); white (*Plain Pastels*)
- **white pen**: Pentel Milky Gel Roller
- **black pen**: Zig® Millenium
- **page designer**: Shauna Berglund-Immel

First Snow Nov 1998

...Daniel and Frosty...

BEND, OREGON

CASSIE, DANIELE AND MATT INNERTUBING

cut 2 arms

It's easy to create a natural, rustic look—great for those camping pages—with torn paper. Glue three overlapping triangles from 2"-3" wide to form trees. Glue a brown trunk to the base of each. We've provided patterns as a guide for tearing, but don't try to be exact—the more irregular the shape, the better. Tear 1" wide brown strips and overlap their ends for a border. Add black penwork to the trees and borders.

- **patterned Paper Pizazz™**: green crackled (*Spattered, Crackled, Sponged*)
- **solid Paper Pizazz™**: brown, green (*Solid Muted Colors*)
- **deckle scissors**: Family Treasures, Inc.
- **metal-edged ruler**
- **black pen**: Zig® Writer
- **page designer**: LeNae Gerig

Torn paper has fuzzy edges, so the technique lends itself especially well to piecing furry animals like this cat. The autumn leaves paper not only matches Louis' costume, it sets an autumn theme for Halloween. Trace and transfer the cat patterns to the back of colored paper. Place the paper on a hard surface, press one finger against the line to control the tear and pull gently with the other hand. Tear black stripes freehand. Glue them to the cat pieces and tear away excess. Glue the cat pieces together as shown. Write "cat," "meow" and "kitty" and doodle paw prints in the border.

- **patterned Paper Pizazz™**: fall leaves (*Holidays & Seasons*, also by the sheet)
- **solid Paper Pizazz™**: brown, orange (*Solid Muted Colors*); black (*Solid Jewel Tones*); pink, white (*Plain Pastels*)
- **deckle scissors**: Family Treasures, Inc.
- **three 12" strands of natural raffia**
- **black pen**: Zig® Writer
- **page designer**: LeNae Gerig

tear 2 front and back paws

tear 2 ears and inner ears

This torn paper snowman is resting in a field of frost torn snowflake vellum. To make him, tear three circles of graduated sizes 2"-3" wide. Trace the scarf and hat patterns onto the back of your paper and gently tear along the lines. Add penwork details using a black pen. Use decorating chalk to give him rosy cheeks—after all, it's chilly out there!

- **patterned Paper Pizazz™**: vellum snow (*Vellum Papers*, also by the sheet); forest green pinstripe, red with tri-dots (*Dots, Checks, Plaids & Stripes*, also by the sheet); denim (*Country*, also by the sheet); ivory crackled (*Textured Papers*, also by the sheet)
- **solid Paper Pizazz™**: black (*Solid Jewel Tones*); white (*Plain Pastels*); peach (*Solid Muted Colors*)
- **pink decorating chalk**: Craf-T Products
- **white pen**: Pentel Milky Gel Roller
- **black pen**: Zig® Writer
- **page designer**: LeNae Gerig

All little bears get sleepy at night, including our cuddly torn paper cub. To make him, transfer the patterns to the back of your paper and gently tear along the lines. Use a black pen to add squiggly outlines and glue together as shown. LeNae used decorating chalk to blush this bear's cheeks just like Molly's.

- **patterned Paper Pizazz™**: gold stars (*A Woman's Scrapbook*, also by the sheet); blue with moon and stars (by the sheet)
- **solid Paper Pizazz™**: pink (*Plain Pastels*); black (*Solid Jewel Tones*); yellow (*Solid Muted Colors*)
- **metal-edged ruler**
- **white pen**: Pentel Milky Gel Roller
- **black pen**: Zig® Writer
- **page designer**: LeNae Gerig

body

Tear 2 arms and paw pads.

Tear 2 legs and foot pads.

Tear 2 ears and 2 inner ears.

97

TEA BAG FOLDING

Tea bag folding is a paper art invented in Holland using the pretty papers wrapping tea bags. Look at the motifs and borders you can create with just a few folds! Unless otherwise stated in the instructions, use 1½" squares.

Diamond fold instructions:
1. Cut the square into an equilateral triangle 1½" wide and 1⅓" high.
2. Fold in half vertically; unfold.
3. Fold in half horizontally; unfold.
4. Place right side down and bring each bottom corner to the horizontal fold as shown. Turn right side up.

Made of tea bag folded diamonds, this page looks like a lovingly stitched quilt. Cut 36 squares each of brown suede and plaid paper. Follow the directions above to fold diamonds. Glue the diamonds into stars as shown on matting paper. Trim the mats, leaving a ¹⁄₁₆" border around each star. Arrange on the page with matted photos.

- **patterned Paper Pizazz™**: yellow/rust plaid (*Jewel Plaids*); crushed suede (*Black & White Photos*); rust/gold plaid (by the sheet)
- **solid Paper Pizazz™**: goldenrod (*Plain Brights*)
- **black pen**: Zig® Writer
- **page designer**: Amy Gustafson

Kite fold instructions:
1. Fold a square in half diagonally to find the center; unfold.
2. Place it right side down and fold in each side to lie against the center line. Turn right side up.

Tea bag folding and paper piecing are combined on this page—the bottom border is a field of tulips made out of tea bag folded kites! Cut 24 green, 12 red and 12 yellow ¾" squares. Fold each into a kite as shown above. (Then pat yourself on the back for folding 48 kites!) Assemble and glue them into tulips as shown.

- **patterned Paper Pizazz™**: blue stripe, yellow swirl, red/yellow plaid, green lattice (*Bright Tints*)
- **solid Paper Pizazz™**: green (*Plain Brights*); light green, white (*Plain Pastels*)
- **black pen**: Sakura Gelly Roll
- **page designer**: Amy Gustafson

This pretty pleated fan made from laser lace echoes the fans in the background paper. And it's trimmed with the same ribbon used to adorn the photo corners, further unifying the page. To make the fan, cut laser lace into six 2½" squares. Fold each square into a kite as shown on page 98. Trim the top point from each kite and glue pieces of ribbon to the top and bottom. Glue the kites into a fan as shown and glue a bow to the point.

- **patterned Paper Pizazz™**: vintage fans (*Vintage Papers*); laser lace (*Romantic Papers*, also by the sheet)
- **solid Paper Pizazz™**: rose, yellow (*Solid Muted Colors*); ivory (*Plain Pastels*)
- **16" of ⅜" wide mint picot ribbon:** Wrights®
- **metallic silver pen:** Pentel Gel Roller
- **page designer:** Amy Gustafson

The vellum tea bag motif decorating this page looks like a bow on a present. For the motif, cut eight 1½" squares from the floral border of purple quilt vellum, and eight ¾" squares from the dotted border of the same sheet. Fold each square into a kite as shown on page 98. Tape the large kites into a circle on white paper and trim, leaving a 1⁄16" border. (Tape is less likely than glue to show through the vellum.) Mat the small kites on white and tape to the motif as shown.

- **patterned Paper Pizazz™**: vellum dots (*Vellum Papers*, also by the sheet); purple quilt vellum (*Colored Vellum Papers*); purple starbursts (*Light Great Backgrounds*)
- **solid Paper Pizazz™**: white (*Plain Pastels*)
- **silver photo corners:** Canson-Talens, Inc.
- **double-stick acid-free tape:** Scotch® Brand
- **purple chisel-tip pen:** Zig ® Writer
- **metallic silver pen:** Pentel Gel Roller
- **page designer:** LeNae Gerig

The three tea bag motifs on this page repeat the pansy embellishment and, along with the laser lace, make a fancy lower border for the beautiful photo. Cut twelve ¾" pansy squares. Fold each into a kite as shown on page 98. Glue the kites into three half circles on green paper and trim, leaving a ¹⁄₁₆" border. Glue to the page as shown.

- **patterned Paper Pizazz**™: tan pansy with border (*Bj's Handpainted Papers*); green handmade (*The Handmade Look*); laser lace (*Romantic Papers*, also by the sheet); 6 pansy tea bag folding squares (*Tea Bag Folding Papers #2*)
- **solid Paper Pizazz**™: ivory (*Solid Pastel Papers*); green (*Solid Muted Colors*)
- **mini-antique Victorian scissors:** Family Treasures, Inc.
- **page designer:** LeNae Gerig

Square folding instructions:
1. Cut a tea bag square in half diagonally, making two triangles.
2. Place one right side down and bring each bottom corner to the top as shown.

These tea bag folds look like brightly colored pinwheels that might easily amuse these children. Cut six 1½" squares each of yellow/black and red/black checkerboard paper. Cut and fold into a square as shown above. Arrange the squares as shown on black and trim, leaving a ¹⁄₁₆" border. Glue each pinwheel to the 1" border strip, which separates two coordinating paper backgrounds—a technique we call wainscotting.

- **patterned Paper Pizazz**™: red and black checks, yellow and black checks, red with black hollow dots, red and black vertical stripe (by the sheet); black with white dots (*Coordinating Colors™ Black & White*, also by the sheet)
- **solid Paper Pizazz**™: yellow (*Plain Brights*); black (*Solid Jewel Tones*); white (*Plain Pastels*)
- **black pen:** Zig® Writer
- **page designer:** Amy Gustafson

Tea bag folding techniques make attractive borders, as you can see on this page. And, just use the same papers to fold another tea bag motif and you have an instantly coordinated layout. For this page, cut nine 1¾" brown swirl squares, cut and fold into a diamond as instructed on page 98. Cut five 1¾" brown crushed suede squares, cut and fold into squares as shown on page 100. Glue the folds as shown with the diamonds on top.

- **patterned Paper Pizazz™**: brown with gold spatter (*Spattered, Crackled, Sponged*); brown and gold swirl, crushed suede (*Black & White Photos*, also by the sheet)
- **solid Paper Pizazz™**: black (*Solid Jewel Tones*); light brown, dark brown (*Solid Muted Colors*)
- **black pen**: Zig® Writer
- **page designer**: LeNae Gerig

The large tea bag motif centered on this page is a sophisticated embellishment that points our attention to the four photos around it. To make it, cut ten tea bag squares. Fold eight into kites as shown on page 98. Cut two squares diagonally into triangles. Fold them into squares as shown in the diagram on page 100. Glue the kites in a circle on white paper and trim, leaving a narrow border. Mat each square on white and glue to the center of the kites.

- **patterned Paper Pizazz™**: blue suede (*Heritage Papers*, also by the sheet); yellow roses (*Blooming Blossoms*, also by the sheet); 12 blue tea bag folding squares (*Tea Bag Folding Papers #2*)
- **solid Paper Pizazz™**: white (*Plain Pastels*)
- **white pen**: Pentel Milky Gel Roller
- **page designer**: LeNae Gerig

PAPER QUILTING

Most of us have a treasured quilt that's comforting, beautiful and full of memories. Those very qualities make quilt themes perfect for scrapbooking. Let the following page ideas open your creativity to the endless possibilities of scrapbook quilting.

Who could resist this cute Valentine all dressed in red and white? Look closely and you'll see the appliqued hearts, matted on red or white and "sewn" on with pen stitching, were inspired by the hearts on this baby's tee-shirt. The striped squares are matted for visual separation from the red-and-white dotted background paper. The two bold patterns work together because they share the same simple color scheme—which is also why they accent the photo wonderfully.

- **patterned Paper Pizazz™**: red with white dots, red/white stripe (*Ho Ho Ho*, also by the sheet);
- **solid Paper Pizazz™**: red (*Plain Brights*); white (*Plain Pastels*)
- **2" wide heart punch**: Marvy® Uchida
- **1¼" wide heart punch**: McGill, Inc.
- **red pen**: Zig® Writer
- **white pen**: Pentel Milky Gel Roller
- **black pen**: Sakura Gelly Roll
- **page designer**: Amy Gustafson

This classic-looking patchwork quilt page is quick to create. Cut 2" patterned or solid squares and glue them around the edge of a white 12"x12" background sheet, leaving a ¹⁄₁₆" border around each one. Center a 7" red square in the page and divide it into quarters with ¼" wide black strips. Crop the photos into circles to contrast with the angles in the rest of the page, thus attracting attention. Add black and white pen stitches to enhance the quilt feel.

- **patterned Paper Pizazz™**: red and white diamonds, red with white tri-dots (*12"x12" Coordinating Colors™ Red & White*); black with large and small white dots (*Heritage Papers*)
- **solid Paper Pizazz™**: black (*Solid Jewel Tones*); white, red (*12"x12" Coordinating Colors™ Red & White*)
- **deckle scissors**: Family Treasures, Inc.
- **white pen**: Pentel Milky Gel Roller
- **black pen**: Zig® Writer
- **page designer**: LeNae Gerig

The bright colors and funky layout of this page give it a contemporary look, with quilting shapes used as journaling plaques that echo the pattern in the background paper. Cut two 2" squares of blue and one of green. Cut the green square in half diagonally. Punch one blue and two green squares, cut them all in half diagonally, and glue to the large shapes as shown. Mat the large shapes on white and glue to the page.

- **patterned Paper Pizazz**™: green and blue tiles (*A Girl's Scrapbook*)
- **solid Paper Pizazz**™: lime green, blue (*Plain Brights*); white (*Plain Pastels*)
- **½" square punch**: Marvy® Uchida
- **black pen**: Zig® Writer
- **page designer**: Susan Cobb

Who knew geometry could be so fun? By playing with different sizes of squares and triangles, you'll create quilt patterns like this one. Cut four 2" blue and white striped squares, four 2" blue squares and two 1" white squares. Cut each diagonally into triangles, and arrange them as shown on white with blue dots paper. The dotted paper turns into a star that frames this sunny photo of Haley.

- **patterned Paper Pizazz**™: blue and white stripe, white with blue dots (*Coordinating Colors*™ *Blue & White*)
- **solid Paper Pizazz**™: blue, white (*Coordinating Colors*™ *Blue & White*)
- **white pen**: Pentel Milky Gel Roller
- **page designer**: Susan Cobb

Paper quilted vellum blocks lend elegance to this lovely heritage photo. Cut four 2" and two ¾" mauve patterned vellum squares, four 1" purple hollow dot vellum squares (then cut two in half diagonally), two 1½" blue heart vellum squares, and one 2⅞" blue vellum square (cut it in half diagonally). Arrange on the pink marbled background paper so the diamond blocks frame the photo. It's easy once you get the hang of it!

- **patterned Paper Pizazz™**: pink marbled (*A Woman's Scrapbook*); purple vellum with hollow dots, mauve floral vellum, blue vellum with hearts (*Colored Vellum Papers*)
- **solid Paper Pizazz™**: dark blue, indigo (*Solid Jewel Tones*)
- **purple pen**: Zig® Writer
- **page designer**: Susan Cobb

This paper-quilted layout leaves plenty of room for photos, journaling blocks and a staggered headline—all supported by a gorgeous combination of blue and green shades of patterned paper. We loved the colorful patchwork-style layout of Nicola's double-page spread so much we selected it as an Honorable Mention in our Autumn Pages With Pizazz™ contest. April is autumn in New Zealand, where Nicola lives.

- **patterned Paper Pizazz™**: green crackled (*Spattered, Crackled, Sponged*); blue textured (*Light Great Backgrounds*)
- **solid Paper Pizazz™**: sage, medium blue (*Solid Muted Colors*); black (*12"x12" Coordinating Colors™ Black & White*); white (*Plain Pastels*)
- **lettering template**: Provo Craft®
- **green and blue colored pencils**: EK Success Ltd.
- **black pen**: Zig® Writer
- **page designer**: Nicola Howard

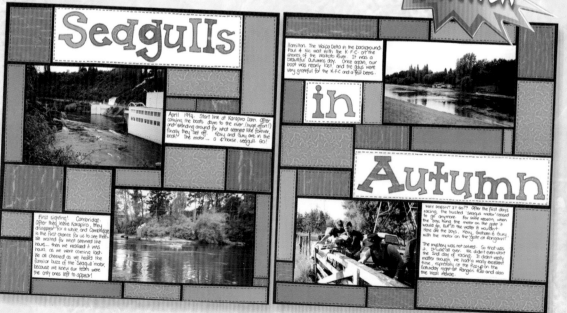

Paper quilted pastel papers form a baby blanket behind this heartwarming photo of baby Brynn. Use the pattern to cut 1" wide strips of five coordinating papers 4", 3" and 2" long. Finish with a 1" square in the center. Make four quilt blocks, then arrange on a different patterned background paper. When selecting your papers, opt for a variety of small patterns that share the same color tones.

- **patterned Paper Pizazz™**: pink/white plaid (*Stripes, Checks & Dots*); blue lines and dots, pink lines and dots, blue/yellow plaid, pink/blue plaid, pink with pastel stripe (*Dots, Checks, Plaids & Stripes*)
- **solid Paper Pizazz™**: yellow (*Solid Muted Colors*); white (*Plain Pastels*)
- **2" wide heart template**: Extra Special Products Corp.
- **metallic silver pen**: Marvy® Uchida
- **page designer**: Amy Gustafson

Teri's sweet paper quilted page is a wonderful combination of patterned papers, vellum overlays and whimsical journaling. We love how Teri matched the paper colors and patterns to those in Elise's dress. The patterned white-on-white and colored vellum overlays on the apples, leaves and journaling squares adds a subtle touch of dimension. Nice job, Teri and congratulations on the Honorable Mention award from our Autumn Pages with Pizazz™ contest. Keep 'em coming, Teri!

- **patterned Paper Pizazz™**: green with stars, green and white stripe, burgundy with tri-dots, green/burgundy plaid (*Dots, Checks, Plaids & Stripes*); green vellum with leaves (*Colored Vellum Papers*); vellum with dots and lines (*Vellum Papers*)
- **solid Paper Pizazz™**: burgundy, hunter green (*Solid Jewel Tones*); white (*Plain Pastels*)
- **1¼" and 1½" scalloped square and 1¼" long leaf punches**: Family Treasures, Inc.
- **School Days stickers**: Debbie Mumm
- **scallop scissors**: Creative Memories
- **Alphabet Soup lettering template**: Provo Craft®
- **page designer**: Teri Cutts

FANCY KNIFEWORK

The following pages feature brand new "fancy knifework". We think they'll provide lots of inspiration as you develop your scrapbook pages.

Doesn't the vellum layered over frosted leaves paper add a touch of autumn frost to the page? The unexpected combination of these two papers, with a purple stardust pattern and barnwood matting plus lettering was so beautiful we awarded it Second Prize on our Autumn Pages With Pizazz™ contest.

- **patterned Paper Pizazz™**: lavender starbursts (*Great Backgrounds*); frosted leaves (*The Great Outdoors,* also by the sheet); barnwood (*Country,* also by the sheet); vellum with ferns (*Vellum Papers,* also by the sheet)
- **solid Paper Pizazz™**: specialty silver (*Pearlescent Papers,* also by the sheet); white (*Plain Pastels*); ivory (*Solid Pastel Papers*)
- **mini-scallop scissors**: Fiskars®, Inc.
- **Classic Capitals lettering template**: Frances Meyer, Inc.
- **scallop ruler**: Creative Memories
- **X-acto® knife and cutting surface**
- **page designer**: Teri Cutts

Take a peek under the flaps to see how Susan combined this wedding photo and invitation into a layout as special as that special day! Cut a sheet of 12"x12" rose paper in half diagonally, making sure the roses will be facing up on the finished page. Trim around the roses on the edges that will extend over the page. Save extra roses to use as embellishments. Mat each flap on yellow paper and attach to the back of the page.

- **patterned Paper Pizazz™**: yellow roses, yellow diamonds (*Soft Florals & Patterns*); 2 sheets laser lace (*Romantic Papers,* also by the sheet)
- **solid Paper Pizazz™**: white, pale yellow (*Solid Pastel Papers*)
- **X-acto® knife and cutting surface**
- **page designer**: Susan Cobb

Bargello is the name for a museum in Florence, Italy, a quilt design, a rubber stamp technique—and now we're bringing it to scrapbooking. Narrow strips of patterned papers, ¼"-½", are arranged in varying directions and glued to paper. Trim the ends of the strips, then mat the Bargello motif and page corners on a contrasting color of paper.

- **patterned Paper Pizazz**™: green diamonds, green chevrons, green swirls (*Soft Tints*)
- **solid Paper Pizazz**™: pale yellow (*Plain Pastels*)
- **X-acto® knife and cutting surface**
- **metal-edged ruler**
- **green pen:** Zig® Writer
- **page designer:** Susan Cobb

Strips of softly patterned papers combine with elegant laser lace paper to beautifully complement the tones of this hand-tinted photo. While the ¼", ⅜" and ½" wide strips vary in size, it's easy to cut them straight with a metal ruler and an X-acto® knife. Arrange the strips on purple solid paper, allowing some of the purple to peek through. Cut into a square, mat on a lavender paper and attach to the background. Notice the background is two patterned papers—the iris paper was also used for the paper strip design. Beautiful!

- **patterned Paper Pizazz**™: purple lattice, soft irises (*Soft Florals & Patterns*); laser lace (*Romantic Papers*, also by the sheet)
- **solid Paper Pizazz**™: lavender, pale lavender (*Solid Muted Colors*); pale yellow, ivory (*Plain Pastels*)
- **X-acto® knife and cutting surface**
- **metal-edged ruler**
- **white pen:** Pentel Milky Gel Roller
- **page designer:** Susan Cobb

The folded colored vellum mat corners are an elegant touch to this beautiful page. Susan folded each edge up ¼" and secured it with double sided tape. Then she added a metallic silver paper strip to accent the fold and hide the tape. She folded the corner back over the silver and then folded the tip of the corner up. And notice how Susan double-matted the photo on lavender paper and stitched patterned vellum, then placed a smaller pink mat under the vellum to create a variety of tones. Simply gorgeous—and perfect for this photo!

- **patterned Paper Pizazz™**: pink and blue with roses (*Collage Papers*); purple lattice vellum (*Colored Vellum Papers*)
- **solid Paper Pizazz™**: pale lavender, pale pink (*Plain Pastels*)
- **9" of ⅝" wide lavender satin ribbon**: Wrights®
- **metallic silver pen**: Zebra® Jimnie® Gel Roller
- **page designer**: Susan Cobb

A wonderful heritage portrait is highlighted with a special folded mat. Susan simply folded up each corner of the black mat ⅜", tucked a gold metallic paper triangle underneath, then folded the black corner tip down to overlap the gold. The black mat was then matted on metallic gold paper, placed on white dotted vellum and accented with gold photo corners. The black and gold papers are perfect for this masculine page.

- **patterned Paper Pizazz™**: spattered with foil and blueberry border (*Bj's Gold & Handpainted Papers*); vellum with dots (*Vellum Papers*)
- **solid Paper Pizazz™**: specialty gold (*Metallic Papers*, also by the sheet); black (*Solid Jewel Tones*)
- **gold photo corners**: Canson-Talens, Inc.
- **metallic gold pen**: Pentel Milky Gel Roller
- **page designer**: Susan Cobb

How dramatic a little art and fold can be! Susan cut ⅜" long notches in the vellum paper (they're spaced ¾" apart) then folded each down. A silver pen lining completes the design. Also notice the silver mats and offset vellum mats. A beautiful page! Or you can make a template by using a ⅜" square punch, or use the tri-dot pattern of the floral vellum paper as a guide.

- **patterned Paper Pizazz™**: white satin (*Our Wedding*); vellum with floral border (by the sheet)
- **solid Paper Pizazz™**: lavender (*Solid Muted Colors*); sky blue vellum, blue lavender vellum (*Pastel Vellum Papers*); specialty silver (*Pearlescent Papers*, also by the sheet)
- **X-acto® knife and cutting surface**
- **metallic silver pen**: Sakura Gelly Roll
- **page designer**: Susan Cobb

A pretty picture is tucked into a painted vellum pocket for a lovely layout! Cut a 7 ¼"x5¾" vellum rectangle, then score the vertical edges about ¼" on each side and fold under. Cut a ½" square to use as a pattern. Draw around the square every ½" down the left side of the vellum pocket. Cut a + in the center of each square to the edges. Fold back the two opposite corners of each square. Cut a ½" square of gold metallic paper; cut each one into fourths, then cut the smaller squares in half diagonally. Glue a triangle to each folded back vellum triangle. Cut a piece of blue satin patterned paper to fit beneath the pocket, folding the vellum edges over the blue paper. Use a gold pen to line the pocket's top edge and for journaling.

- **patterned Paper Pizazz™**: yellow roses (*Romantic Papers*); blue satin (*Bright Great Backgrounds*); butterfly vellum (*Floral Vellum*)
- **solid Paper Pizazz™**: specialty gold (*Metallic Papers*, also by the sheet); pale yellow (*Plain Pastels*)
- **X-acto® knife and cutting surface**
- **metallic gold pen**: Sakura Gelly Roll
- **page designer**: Susan Cobb

Here's something new! A lattice-cut vellum photo mat adds an extra touch of elegance. Susan started with a 6"x7½" piece of peach vellum. She made 1½" diagonal cuts in the vellum, beginning at the top left corner and cutting every ½" down the left side. She turned the first strip down to the bottom left corner of the next strip, continuing to the bottom edge of the mat, then trimmed the excess at the bottom edge. The collage patterned paper subtly fills the rest of the page. Gold handmade paper, crushed and then smoothed, and a coordinating bow complete the layout.

- **patterned Paper Pizazz™**: peach/yellow collage (*Collage Papers*); peach vellum with dots and border (*Colored Vellum Papers*)
- **solid Paper Pizazz™**: yellow, brown (*Solid Muted Colors*)
- **gold handmade paper**
- **gold photo corners**: Canson-Talens, Inc.
- **9" of ⅝" wide gold mesh ribbon**: Wright's®
- **X-acto® knife and cutting surface**
- **metal-edged ruler**
- **metallic gold pen**: Zebra® Jimnie® Gel Rollerball
- **page designer**: Susan Cobb

The folded cross-hatch photo corners draw attention to the photo—and coordinate perfectly with the metallic gold lattice border on the background paper! Double mat the photo, leaving the second mat about ⅜" wide. Glue two 2" squares of metallic gold paper to the back of the photo mat at the top left and lower right corners. At each of these corners, make a ⅜" deep cut in the corner and ¼" to each side of the corner, creating two ¼" wide strips. Make another ⅜" deep cut on each side of these strips, creating two ⅜" wide strips (see the diagram). Fold the two narrow strips to overlap in an "X" over the corner of the photo. Fold the remaining strips out to the edge of the blue mat and glue in place. Clever lady, Susan!

- **patterned Paper Pizazz™**: daisies (*Bj's Gold & Handpainted Papers*)
- **solid Paper Pizazz™**: pale yellow (*Plain Pastels*); blue (*Solid Muted Colors*); specialty gold (*Metallic Papers*, also by the sheet)
- **oval die-cut**: Ellison® Craft & Design
- **metallic gold pen**: Zebra® Jimnie® Gel Rollerball
- **page designer**: Susan Cobb

Paper embroidery is a technique new to scrap-booking—and a lovely way to highlight a heritage photo. To create these embroidered stars, transfer the pattern to your paper, then poke a pinhole at each dot. Follow these instructions, pulling the threaded needle gently through the paper.

black arrows = stitches on front of paper
purple arrows = stitches on back of paper

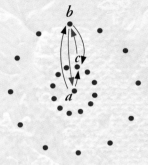

1. *Up through a, down through b*
2. *Up through a, down through c*
3. *Up through b, down through c*
4. *Repeat, moving clockwise around the circle.*

- **patterned Paper Pizazz™**: brown/green with border collage (*Collage Papers*); brown hand-made, ivory handmade (*"Handmade" Papers*)
- **solid Paper Pizazz™**: sage green vellum (*Pastel Vellum Papers*); mauve (*Solid Muted Colors*)
- **gold handmade paper**

- **48" of metallic gold thread**: Westrim® Crafts
- **sewing needle**
- **metallic gold pen**: Sakura Gelly Roll
- **page designer**: Susan Cobb

A vellum waterfall-folded embellishment is a lovely touch to this delicate page. To create your own waterfall-folded embellishment, cut a 4" pastel vellum square and fold into fourths. Turn so the open corner is at the top. Fold the layers down one at a time, folding each point ⅛" shorter than the previous one. Edge each flap with a metallic gold pen, add a vellum floral cut-out and attach a satin bow. Notice the same pastel vellum is used to mat the photos. The roses are cut from the vellum sheet and beautifully fill the page corners.

- **patterned Paper Pizazz™**: white satin (*Wedding*, also by the sheet); rose vellum (*Floral Vellum*)
- **solid Paper Pizazz™**: pale yellow (*Plain Pastels*); pale green (*Solid Muted Colors*); coral vellum (*Pastel Vellum Papers*)
- **8" of ¼" wide ivory satin ribbon**: Wrights
- **metallic gold pen**: Sakura Gelly Roll
- **page designer**: Susan Cobb

AMBERLY

1998

BAKE

Christopher's 1st Birthday was also his very first piece of chocolate cake October 19, 1997

October 2001

FUN TECHNIQUES

This final chapter is a wonderful mix of new ideas and fresh looks at scrapbooking. Let's begin with newer tools like a circle cutter, oval cutter and paper corrugator. Our goal is to provide you with some new ideas to go with these new toys.

Recipes make great additions to scrapbooks. They're often part of a memory or associated with someone we love. Here are eight clever ways to incorporate recipes into your album.

Okay, no matter how hard you try, sometimes you simply miss getting a photograph of an event. Never fear, scrapbook the memory anyway! On pages 124-127 you'll find some options to get you started.

"Creating a scene" is not throwing a tantrum! Rather, it's using papers to create a scene that's simply perfect for your photos. You become the artist (it's okay, we're here to help) and we'll show you how.

Pages with movable parts, even dangles, offer another creative option for scrapbookers. There is no one way to make a movable, dangling page but we'll give you 16 ideas to give you inspiration to make your own.

There is a wonderful thing about scrapbooking (okay there are several). But our very favorite is that you are the only judge about what is good in your album. You decide if your pages are simple, more involved, take ten minutes to make or may take hours (even days). It's all up to you. And, get this, whatever you decide is RIGHT, it's BEST, it's TERRIFIC! All because it belongs to you. We think you're the most important component in your album pages. Why? Because without your effort, without your creativity, none of these precious memories would have been so carefully, so lovingly crafted. You are creating a legacy, one page at a time. And we think you're terrific!!

And to celebrate your work, here is a Scrapbookers Bill of Rights written by Sara Naumann, Marketing Director at Hot Off The Press. It captures our feelings about scrapbookers and we hope you enjoy it.

FUN TOOLS

Circle cutters, oval cutters and paper corrugators are some of the newer scrapbooking supplies. Let's see some ideas using them…

A circle cutter is a wonderful tool for cropping photos—but look at what a little creative cutting can do for your layout! LeNae taped her three rectangular photos to the cutting mat in layout order, then used the circle cutter to cut away half a circle from the photos. The result is a unique layout that draws attention to the round photo on the right (which she also cut with the circle cutter).

- **patterned Paper Pizazz™**: peach floral, green checks (*Soft Florals & Patterns*)
- **solid Paper Pizazz™**: peach (*Solid Muted Colors*); ivory (*Plain Pastels*)
- **⅛" hole punch**: Fiskars®, Inc.
- **seagull scissors**: Fiskars®, Inc.
- **circle cutter**: Fiskars®, Inc.
- **cutting surface**
- **peach and pink photo tinting pens**: EK Success Ltd.
- **foam mounting tape**: Scotch® Brand
- **metallic silver pen**: Pentel Gel Roller
- **page designer**: LeNae Gerig

Can you believe this fun multicolored border was created with a circle cutter? Simply cut two circles of the same size, one from green paper and another from pink. Cut each circle into fourths, then arrange the cut pieces into a border and decorate with punched sun shapes and penwork.

- **patterned Paper Pizazz™**: pink check, yellow check, green dot (*Bright Tints*)
- **solid Paper Pizazz™**: white, pink (*Plain Pastels*); green (*Plain Brights*)
- **medium and large sun punches**: Family Treasures, Inc.
- **small sun punch**: Marvy® Uchida
- **deckle scissors**: Family Treasures, Inc.
- **black fine-tip and calligraphy pens**: Zig® Writer
- **page designer**: LeNae Gerig

Circles in squares—what a creative way to crop a photo to focus on the central image, without eliminating background that's needed to set the mood! The circle cutter was used to carefully cut out the center of the photo. The remaining square was then cut in fourths, and all the pieces were matted slightly apart on plain white paper to look like they're centered in a lens. The corner punches on the black mats add to the focused effect.

- **patterned Paper Pizazz**™: characters with pencils, Donald cut-outs (*Disney's Playtime with Mickey and Friends*)
- **solid Paper Pizazz**™: dark blue (*Solid Jewel Tones*); white (*Solid Pastels*)
- **Punch-Outs**™: pencil (*School Punch Outs*™)
- **corner slot punch**: Family Treasures, Inc.
- **circle cutter**: Fiskars®, Inc.
- **deckle scissors**: Family Treasures, Inc.
- **blue pen**: Zig®
- **page designer**: Debbie Peterson

Disney characters ©Disney Enterprises, Inc.
Used by permission from Disney Enterprises, Inc.

For this page the oval cutter was used to make a border of bunting swags as well as to crop the photos. For each swag loop, just cut half an oval (ours are 4" wide), then reduce the cutter size slightly and cut away the top of the oval, forming a crescent. Each loop is composed of a blue crescent overlapped on a dotted and a white one. Punched stars hide the uneven ends and add a festive touch.

- **patterned Paper Pizazz**™: Pooh parade (*Disney's Special Days with Pooh*); white dots on red (*Ho Ho Ho!!!*, also by the sheet); blue stars (*Birthday Time!*)
- **solid Paper Pizazz**™: white (*Plain Pastels*); red, blue, yellow (*Plain Brights*)
- **Punch-Outs**™: dancing Pooh, dancing Tigger, Piglet with balloon, Eeyore (*Disney's Pooh Punch-Outs*™)
- **star punches**: Marvy® Uchida
- **oval cutter**: Fiskars®, Inc.
- **stamp, ripple long scissors**: Fiskars®, Inc.
- **black pen**: Zig®
- **page designer**: LeNae Gerig

Disney characters ©Disney Enterprises, Inc.
Used by permission from Disney Enterprises, Inc.

Corrugated photo mats add dimension to this formal page. This corrugator crimps the paper into a wavy pattern to nicely frame the silhouette-cut photos. Use an X-acto® knife to slit a few portions of the ivy border so it overlaps the photo.

- **patterned Paper Pizazz™**: vine border (*Bj's Handpainted Papers*)
- **solid Paper Pizazz™**: red, dark green (*Solid Jewel Tones*); white (*Plain Pastels*)
- **letter stickers**: Making Memories
- **mini-scallop-and-point scissors**: Provo Craft®
- **oval cutter**: Fiskars®, Inc.
- **wave paper corrugator**: Paper Adventures
- **page designer**: Debbie Peterson

Running the paper through the corrugator, then giving the paper a quarter turn to corrugate it again sideways results in a unique cross-hatch effect. The look combines nicely with the green and brown color combination to support the outdoor theme of the page. *Note*: Punch the leaves after you've run them through the corrugator—it's much easier than trying to fit the tiny pieces through!

- **patterned Paper Pizazz™**: green velvet (*"Velvet" Backgrounds*); oatmeal handmade (*Solid Muted Colors*)
- **solid Paper Pizazz™**: brown (*Solid Muted Colors*)
- **leaf border punch**: All Night Media®, Inc.
- **½" wide leaf punch**: E-maginations Crafts
- **½" and 7/8" scalloped square punches, Victorian corner punch**: Family Treasures, Inc.
- **letter stickers**: Provo Craft®
- **deckle scissors**: Family Treasures, Inc.
- **paper corrugator**: Fiskars®, Inc.
- **page designer**: Debbie Peterson

Corrugated blue squares are the perfect place to put these fun paper pieced frogs! The green frogs match the frogs in the patterned background paper; the blue squares, plus the blue photo mats, add color to the page. And corrugating the black photo mats and the journaling square add additional dimension and help to balance the page.

- **patterned Paper Pizazz™**: friendly bugs (*Child's Play*, also by the sheet); green with white dots (*Christmas*, also by the sheet)
- **solid Paper Pizazz™**: black (*Solid Jewel Tones*); blue (*Plain Brights*); white (*Plain Pastels*)
- **letter stickers**: Making Memories™
- **long scallop scissors**: Fiskars®, Inc.
- **paper corrugator**: Marvy® Uchida
- **green pen**: Zig® Writer
- **page designer**: LeNae Gerig

Here the corrugated photo mats and border squares combine with heart-shaped buttons and a classic color combination to present a pretty, country theme. A sheer ribbon links one border square to the next and supports the clever journaling. Crimping the paper so the wales run vertically helps to lead the viewer's eye to the journaling plaque.

- **patterned Paper Pizazz™**: navy with white pinstripes, burgundy with tri-dots (*Dots, Checks, Plaids, & Stripes*, also by the sheet)
- **solid Paper Pizazz™**: pale yellow (*Plain Pastels*)
- **paper corrugator**: Marvy® Uchida
- **buttons**: Dress It Up®
- **12" of ¼" wide sheer white ribbon**: Wrights®
- **blue pen**: Zebra Pen Corporation
- **page designer**: Amy Gustafson

Corrugate 1/2"-wide strips of green paper, then weave them with plain rose-colored paper strips to create this pretty heart. And because the background paper is bordered with butterflies, the heart embellishment is the only decoration needed to highlight the photo. Just think of the possibilities—can't you see this heart made from pastel papers to decorate a baby page, or made from red and pink for Valentine's Day?

- **patterned Paper Pizazz™**: blue stripes with butterfly border, mauve stripes (*Perfect Pairs™ Blue & Raspberry*)
- **solid Paper Pizazz™**: mauve (*Perfect Pairs™ Blue & Raspberry*); white (*Plain Pastels*); green (*Solid Jewel Tones*); muted green (*Solid Muted Colors*)
- **deckle scissors**: Family Treasures, Inc.
- **paper corrugator**: Fiskars®, Inc.
- **page designer**: Debbie Peterson

A checkerboard effect is just perfect for this chess-themed page! Weave eight 1"-wide black paper strips with six 1"-wide green diamond strips to create this checkerboard mat. Start by placing a green strip over a black strip to form an "L" shape; continue adding and weaving the strips. Add black strips around the edge of the woven area to finish the sides.

- **patterned Paper Pizazz™**: green diamonds (*Perfect Pairs™ Blue & Raspberry*)
- **solid Paper Pizazz™**: black (*Solid Jewel Tones*); green (*Perfect Pairs™ Blue & Raspberry*); white (*Plain Pastels*)
- **corner rounder punch**: Family Treasures, Inc.
- **deckle scissors**: Family Treasures, Inc.
- **paper corrugator**: Fiskars®, Inc.
- **page designer**: Debbie Peterson

A corrugator can even create a wonderful lace look to match the lace of the baby's christening gown. The white photo mat was corrugated, then edged with patterned scissors and hole punched for a lace-trimmed effect. The borders at the top and bottom of the page were created the same way, then threaded with a pink satin ribbon to separate the two patterned papers while creating a frame for the photo. Such a dear page!

- **patterned Paper Pizazz™**: pink with white stitches, pink/yellow plaid (*Making Heritage Scrapbook Pages*, plaid paper also by the sheet)
- **solid Paper Pizazz™**: white (*Plain Pastels*); yellow (*Solid Muted Colors*)
- **cloud scissors**: Fiskars®, Inc.
- **¹⁄₁₆" hole punch**: McGill, Inc.
- **paper corrugator**: Fiskars®, Inc.
- **ribbon**: 24" of ¼" wide pink satin by Wrights®
- **black pen**: Sakura of America
- **page designer**: Amy Gustafson

A tidal wave of fun! Running wave die-cuts through a corrugator adds a dimensional look to these page embellishments. Just be sure that the corrugated pattern runs the same direction on all the die-cuts. Let a few of the die-cut waves splash over one of the photos to lend additional dimension to the layout. Pink patterned papers are a perfect backdrop to all the blue in the photos yet still reflect feminine Molly.

- **patterned Paper Pizazz™**: pink with white flowers, pink plaid (*Coordinating Colors™ Pink & White*)
- **solid Paper Pizazz™**: blue, white (*Plain Pastels*); white (*Coordinating Colors™ Pink & White*)
- **wave die-cut**: Accu/Cut® Systems, Inc.
- **orca and water splash stickers**: Mrs. Grossman's Paper Company®
- **seagull scissors**: Fiskars®, Inc.
- **paper corrugator**: Fiskars®, Inc.
- **black pen**: Zig® Writer
- **page designer**: LeNae Gerig

© & ™Accu/Cut® Systems

FOOD RECIPES

Recipes are a wonderful part of scrapbooking, sometimes they're even written in the cook's own handwriting. They're always close to our hearts (and not far from our tummies). Here are some ideas.

Slip a receipe in a pocket on your page and it can become a moveable part! Pumpkin patterned paper colors reinforce the theme of this page and Punch-Outs™ add a quick embellishment.

- **patterned Paper Pizazz™**: red with yellow spirals, red/yellow plaid (*Bright Tints*)
- **solid Paper Pizazz™**: white (*Plain Pastels*); yellow (*Solid Muted Colors*)
- **"Give Thanks", pumpkin and turkey Punch-Outs™**: *Annie's Kids Punch-Outs™*
- **scallop ruler**: C-Thru® Ruler Co.
- **black pen**: Zig® Writer
- **page designer**: Shauna Berglund-Immel

Here's a sweet way to preserve a family recipe—along with photos of the event! Simply mat the recipe card to the red border and add a journaling plaque to the top area. The sugar cookies embellishing the border were made by layering patterned vellum on top of yellow circle punched pieces, then decorated with multicolored sprinkles to match the sugar cookies in the background paper. Notice how some of the cookies in the background paper have been slit with an X-acto® knife to overlap the matted photos.

- **patterned Paper Pizazz™**: sugar cookies (*Yummy Papers*); red with white dots (*Christmas Time*); vellum with tri-dots (*Vellum Papers*, also by the sheet)
- **solid Paper Pizazz™**: white, light blue, aqua blue (*Solid Pastel Papers*); black (*Solid Jewel Tones*); yellow (*Solid Muted Colors*); red (*Plain Brights*)
- **1" circle punch**: Family Treasures, Inc.
- **seagull scissors**: Family Treasures, Inc.
- **Fat Caps alphabet template**: Francis Meyer, Inc.
- **recipe card**: Current, Inc.
- **black pen**: Zig® Writer
- **page designer**: LeNae Gerig

Scrapbooking a recipe from an event like a baby shower/tea party adds a special memory to an album. Print the recipe on white paper, then add black dotted background paper to the bottom two-thirds of the page. A punch art border hides the seam between the two papers and a paper pieced teapot overlaps the photo and balances the page. Pattern for the teapot is on page 142.

- **patterned Paper Pizazz™**: black with white dots (by the sheet); green with white dots (*Christmas*, also by the sheet)
- **solid Paper Pizazz™**: red, blue, aqua, orange, fuchsia, golden-rod, green (*Plain Brights*); white, pink (*Plain Pastels*)
- **¼" hole punch**: McGill, Inc.
- **1" and ⅝" circle punches and 1" long leaf punch**: Family Treasures, Inc.
- **teapot die-cut**: Accu/Cut® Systems, Inc.
- **deckle scissors**: Family Treasures, Inc.
- **black pen**: Zig® Writer
- **page designer**: LeNae Gerig

When scrapbooking pages of the children, don't forget to include memories of their favorite treats! A recipe for Bon Bon Peppermint Pie is matted on—what else?—red and white striped paper, then tucked inside a snowflake-patterned vellum envelope matted on red. This layout is perfect for including the cook's own handwriting and the recipe can be removed from the album. The peppermint candy embellishments are cut right from the background paper—just be sure to cut them with an X-acto® knife from the area where the photos will cover the holes. The pattern for the envelope is on page 142.

- **patterned Paper Pizazz™**: peppermint candies (*Yummy Papers*); red and white stripe (*Ho Ho Ho!!!*, also by the sheet); vellum with snowflakes (*Vellum Papers*, also by the sheet) only buy one sheet
- **solid Paper Pizazz™**: red (*Plain Brights*); white (*Plain Pastels*)
- **envelope die-cut**: Accu/Cut® Systems, Inc.
- **mini-scallop scissors**: Fiskars®, Inc.
- **black pen**: Marvy® Uchida
- **pop dots**: All Night Media®
- **page designer**: Shauna Berglund-Immel

A recipe page is a wonderful way to honor a family member's favorite (or famous!) recipe. A section of chips were cut from a sheet of chip-patterned paper, then layered with individually-cut chips attached with foam tape. The olives, onions and chives are punched pieces. Using lettering templates to cut titling letters is a great way to use the rest of the patterned paper, and ties the page together.

- **patterned Paper Pizazz™**: blue with check border (*Bj's Handpainted Papers*); corn chips (*Yummy Papers*); ivory crackle (*Textured Papers*)
- **solid Paper Pizazz™**: burgundy, black (*Solid Jewel Tones*); goldenrod (*Plain Brights*); white, ivory (*Plain Pastels*)
- **½" circle, Mexican border punches**: McGill, Inc.
- **¼" hole, ³/8" long rectangle border, ³/8" square punches**: Marvy® Uchida
- **ABC Tracers template**: EK Success Ltd.
- **foam tape**: All Night Media® Pop Dots
- **page designer**: Shauna Berglund-Immel

Not every recipe page has to include a formal recipe—sometimes it's fun to journal the way the kids make a snack! The combination of graham crackers cut from a patterned paper, and a chocolate chunk background design are perfect for scrapbooking this favorite "recipe".

- **patterned Paper Pizazz™**: chocolate chunks, graham crackers (*Yummy Papers*); brown plaid (*The Great Outdoors*)
- **solid Paper Pizazz™**: white (*Plain Pastels*)
- **corkscrew scissors**: Fiskars®, Inc.
- **white pen**: Pentel Milky Gel Roller
- **black pen**: Marvy® Uchida
- **page designer**: Shauna Berglund-Immel

A child's first birthday cake is always a memorable experience—and often, it's a messy one too! A cake slice die-cut is decorated with "frosting" to provide a clever journaling space, while chocolate chunk die-cut letters add to the theme. The star patterned background paper, and the red striped photo mats, give a touch of color and emphasize the fun of this event. The cake pattern is on page 66.

- **patterned Paper Pizazz**™: red with white stars, red and white stripe (*Stripes, Checks & Dots*); chocolate chunks (*Yummy Papers*)
- **solid Paper Pizazz**™: black (*Solid Jewel Tones*); white, ivory (*Solid Pastel Papers*)
- **cake slice and letter die-cuts:** Accu/Cut® Systems, Inc.
- **black pen:** Zig® Writer
- **foam mounting tape:** Scotch® Brand
- **page designer:** LeNae Gerig

Vellum and silver metallic papers become a "glass" cereal bowl and a silver spoon—the perfect embellishments for this fun page! The cereal paper was silhouette-cut and attached to a solid yellow background paper; a few individual fruit loops were cut from the paper with an X-acto® knife and added to the page with foam tape. The vellum glass bowl lets some of the cereal show through while providing a fun way to frame the matted photo. The spoon is positioned to "point" to the photo. The pattern for the spoon and bowl is on page 142.

- **patterned Paper Pizazz**™: fruit-flavored O's cereal (*Yummy Papers*)
- **solid Paper Pizazz**™: blue (*Plain Brights*); white (*Plain Pastels*); sky blue vellum (*Pastel Vellum*); specialty silver (*Pearlescent Papers*, also by the sheet); yellow (*Solid Plain Pastels*)
- **boy eating cereal, "Smile" Punch-Outs**™: *Annie's Kids Punch-Outs*™
- **bear paper embosser:** Marvy® Uchida
- **letter die-cuts:** Accu/Cut® Systems, Inc.
- **black pen:** Zig® Writer
- **page designer:** Shauna Berglund-Immel

IF YOU MISS THE PHOTO...

...scrapbook the memory! An album can display many mementoes other than photographs. Just one caution: If you're not sure the article is acid-free and lignin-free, be sure to make a color photocopy on acid-free paper rather than using the original in the album.

A letter of appreciation such as this one needs to be displayed with pride, rather than tucked away in a file cabinet and forgotten. Mounted on a pretty patterned paper and embellished with school related Punch-Outs™, it can be enjoyed repeatedly. The explanation (done in printer script on a "blackboard") on the facing page tells us why the letter is important.

If you have related photos, too, these would also make a good cover page or introduction to a theme album about your activities.

- **patterned Paper Pizazz™**: green plaid, burgundy with white tri-dots (*Stripes, Checks & Dots*)
- **solid Paper Pizazz™**: white (*Plain Pastels*); white (*Solid Pastel Papers*); black (*Solid Jewel Tones*)
- **crayon, birdhouse, bear, girl and angel Punch-Outs™**: *Country Friends Punch-Outs™*
- **sunflower scissors**: Fiskars®, Inc.
- **white pen**: Pentel of America
- **black pen**: Zig® Writer
- **page designer**: Amberly Beck

In the anguish and stress of a loved one's last illness, we may not have time for photos. Or, even if we do, they may not represent positive memories we want to linger over. In such a situation, do as LeNae did and scrapbook a special page with a favorite photo from happier times. Journal the necessary details but put the emphasis on the good shared memories which LeNae will now pass on to her daughter.

- **patterned Paper Pizazz™**: black with watercolor roses, black with watercolor roses border (*Watercolor Florals*); peach moiré (*Black & White Photos*)
- **solid Paper Pizazz™**: black (*Solid Jewel Tones*); green (*Solid Muted Colors*)
- **X-acto® knive and cutting surface**
- **page designer**: LeNae Gerig

Tell the story with the journaling, then illustrate it with a related photo from a different time. Mommy was too busy consoling Lauren the day she bumped her head to worry about taking pictures. She used a photo of Lauren crawling and made a paper-doll illustration with a tiny band-aid cut from a hidden area of the background paper. The "Ouch!" paper is perfect for this page!

- **patterned Paper Pizazz™**: ouch (*Childhood*, also by the sheet); yellow diamonds, blue checks (*Bright Tints*)
- **solid Paper Pizazz™**: black (*Solid Jewel Tones*); aqua (*Plain Brights*); white, pink, tan (*Plain Pastels*)
- **brown and pink colored pencils**: EK Success Ltd.
- **pink decorating chalk**: Craf-T Products
- **black pen**: Zig® Writer
- **page designer**: LeNae Gerig

They **intended** to take the camera—how many times has that happened to you? All is not lost. The ticket to the baseball game makes a fine souvenir (this, of course, is a photocopy). A picture of Joseph at the same age, scrapbooked with baseball-themed paper and embellishments, will bring back all the memories of that special first game.

- **patterned Paper Pizazz™**: grass (*Pets*, also by the sheet); baseballs (*Sports*, also by the sheet)
- **solid Paper Pizazz™**: red, blue (*Plain Brights*); black (*Solid Jewel Tones*); white (*Plain Pastels*)
- **1" circle punch**: Family Treasures, Inc.
- **red pen**: Zig® Writer
- **page designer**: LeNae Gerig

Concerts are memorable occasions, but taking pictures may be frowned upon even if not specifically forbidden. This clever page reads like a storyboard of the two girls' concert adventure, with each step of their experience journaled and illustrated in a different way. A photocopy of the performer's autograph is the only item that actually came from the event, but there is nothing missing from these memories! The car pattern is on page 143.

- **patterned Paper Pizazz**™: barnwood (*Country*, also by the sheet); brick wall (by the sheet); plain vellum (*Vellum Papers*)
- **solid Paper Pizazz**™: red, yellow, blue (*Plain Brights*), white (*Plain Pastels*)
- **car die-cut**: Accu/Cut® Systems
- **¹/₂" heart, ³/₄"star, ¹/₂" circle punchs**: Marvy® Uchida
- **¹/₂" star** : Family Treasures, Inc.
- **stamp scissors**: Fiskars®, Inc.
- **black pen**: Zig® Millenium
- **yellow pen** : Zig® Brush and Scroll
- **red pen**: Zig® Writer
- **white pen**: Pentel Milky Gel Roller
- **page designer**: Amy Gustafson

Darn, the camera batteries were dead. But this Thanksgiving memory was too special not to scrapbook, so here are a pair of lovely Thanksgiving pages with no photos at all. One features the menu for the meal (with each person's special contribution) and a guest list which reads like a family who's who. The gorgeous "Family"and "Memories" vellum papers have found the perfect background with frosted leaves and letters patterned papers.

- **patterned Paper Pizazz**™: family, memories (*Heritage Vellum*); frosted leaves (*The Great Outdoors*, also by the sheet); letters (*Black & White Photos*, also by the sheet)
- **solid Paper Pizazz**™: white (*Plain Pastels*); specialty gold (*Metallic Papers*, also by the sheet)
- **deckle scissors**: Family Treasures, Inc.
- **metallic gold pen**: Sakura Gelly Roll
- **black pen**: Marvy® Uchida Medallion
- **page designer**: Shauna Berglund-Immel

Collect clippings from your team's season and make a "sports page" with a headline patterned paper and a background of balls (baseballs, footballs, soccer etc. are also available). Shauna pieced two basketball papers to fill her 12"x12" page, hiding the seam along the edge of her photocopied clippings.

- **patterned Paper Pizazz**™: sports page (*Headlines*); basketballs (*Sports*, also by the sheet)
- **solid Paper Pizazz**™: black (*Solid Jewel Tones*)
- **page designer**: Shauna Bergland-Immel

Oops, we forgot the camera! For a long holiday weekend, use a map to show where you went. Keep a journal of your holiday activities and write a paragraph or two for each one. Mat them separately and overlap them on the page. For this beach vacation the sponged patterned paper has the look of a sandy beach; it's easy to imagine walking along discovering the starfish.

- **patterned Paper Pizazz**™: gold sponged, star plaque (*A Woman's Scrapbook*)
- **solid Paper Pizazz**™: cream, ivory, light blue (*Plain Pastels*)
- **starfish die-cut**: Accu/Cut® Systems
- **black pen**: Zig® Millenium
- **yellow, orange, blue and brown decorating chalks**: Craf-T Products
- **map**: ©Rand McNally
- **page designer**: LeNae Gerig

CREATING A SCENE

Cut and paste from different papers to create a background that perfectly matches your occasion.

A misty transparent green vellum sheet creates a watery look and softens the transition between the beach paper used for the ocean floor and the fish paper used for the upper background. Some seaweed, shells and fish were cut from the papers and glued to the front of the vellum to add depth. Vellum bubbles are a great finishing touch.

- **patterned Paper Pizazz**™: sand, seaweed (*Vacation #2*); fish from ocean floor paper (*Vacation*, also by the sheet)
- **solid Paper Pizazz**™: green vellum, yellow vellum (*Pastel Vellum Papers*); light blue, white (*Plain Pastels*)
- **fish Punch-Outs**™: *Vacation Punch-Outs*™
- **deckle scissors**: Family Treasures, Inc.
- **black pen**: Marvy® Uchida Artist
- **foam mounting tape**: Scotch® Brand
- **page designer**: Shauna Berglund-Immel

A wedge-shaped section of bricks cut from one patterned paper leads right into the road in the photo with the sponged "grass" growing into the bricks as it mats the photo. The background paper is actually a border sheet, but with the bottom covered it looks like a trellis or arbor around the photo. The stones and flowers were mounted on foam tape to bring them forward from the fence. The fence pattern on page 21.

- **patterned Paper Pizazz**™: barnwood (*Country*, also by the sheet); cobble stone (by the sheet); beach pebbles (by the sheet); arbor border, green marble (*A Woman's Scrapbook*)
- **solid Paper Pizazz**™: tan (*Solid Muted Colors*)
- **Punch-Outs**™: flowers (*A Woman's Punch-Outs*™)
- **fence die-cut**: Accu/Cut® Systems
- **black pen**: Marvy® Uchida Medallion
- **foam mounting tape**: Scotch® Brand
- **page designer**: Shauna Berglund-Immel

A deckled edge gives a natural line to the grass paper where it meets the sky. The sand traps were cut from stucco paper to mimic the ones in the photos (and to break up the expanse of all that grass). Doesn't the little golfer Punch-Out™ look like he's having more fun than Chuck and Dave right now? At least he's on the green! Golf balls cut from patterned paper are cut and attached with foam dots.

- **patterned Paper Pizazz™**: golf balls (*Sports*, also by the sheet); yellow/black check (*Bold & Bright*, also by the sheet); 12"x12" grass (by the sheet); clouds (*Our Vacation*, also by the sheet); sand (*Textured Papers*)
- **solid Paper Pizazz™**: black (*Solid Jewel Tones*); white (*Plain Pastels*); red, yellow (*Plain Brights*)
- **Punch-Outs™**: paper doll (*Paper Dolls #2*)
- **flag template**: C-Thru® Ruler Co.
- **oval punch**: Family Treasures, Inc.
- **deckle scissors**: Fiskars®
- **black pen**: Marvy® Uchida Medallion
- **white alpha stickers**: Making Memories™
- **foam mounting tape**: Scotch® Brand
- **page designer**: Shauna Bergland-Immel

Susan used tracing paper to copy the faces from the photos, then moved the tracing around on the ivy paper to determine what leaves to cut out. The photos were glued to the back of the cut-out areas. Look closely at the hand extending from a slit in the leaves. The bug jar, cut from a plain area of the vellum cut-outs page, fits into the fingers and holds another ladybug! Very clever, Susan!

- **patterned Paper Pizazz™**: ivy (*Floral Papers*)
- **solid Paper Pizazz™**: green (*Solid Muted Colors*); white (*Plain Pastels*); red (*Plain Brights*)
- **Cut-Outs™**: vellum bugs (*Vellum Cut-Outs™*)
- **yellow pen**: Pentel Milky Gel Roller
- **black pen**: Zig® Millenium
- **X-acto knife and cutting surface**
- **page designer**: Susan Cobb

A clear, moonlit night is perfect for trick-or-treating. This realistic scene was built by adding grass to the bottom of the starry night paper and placing a die-cut tree in the foreground. The mat around Mitchel's silhouetted photo was cut wide to form a cape. A simple oval of yellow paper forms the moon. Following through with the bat theme, the designer chose to place one of the photos upside down, as though Mitchel is hanging from the tree branch. How creative! The tree pattern is on page 142.

- **patterned Paper Pizazz™**: starry night (by the sheet); grass (*Pets,* also by the sheet)
- **solid Paper Pizazz™**: yellow (*Plain Pastels*); black (*Solid Jewel Tones*)
- **tree and bat die-cut**: Accu/Cut® Systems, Inc.
- **deckle scissors**: Family Treasures, Inc.
- **black pen**: Zig® Writer
- **white pen**: Pentel Milky Gel Roller
- **page designer**: LeNae Gerig

© & ™ Accu/Cut® Systems

This page was so simple to make, yet so stunning with its velvet drapes and black forestage. Black chalk was used to create the effect of vertical folds in the theatre curtains. A wide black mat surrounding both photos pulls them back into the stage area. Very effective!

- **patterned Paper Pizazz™**: burgundy velvet (*Velvet Backgrounds*); black with gold border (*For Black & White Photos*)
- **solid Paper Pizazz™**: specialty gold (*Metallic Papers,* also by the sheet); black (*Solid Jewel Tones*)
- **ripple-edged ruler**: Market USA
- **black decorating chalk**: Craf-T Products
- **metallic gold pen**: Sakura Gelly Roll
- **page designer**: Amy Gustafson

Three torn strips of brown paper make a realistic plowed field to tuck these pumpkins into (they're really balloon and apple punches, but who's tellin'?). Cutting along the bottom and top of the barn door lets it open to reveal Lauren inside. (The barn is from an 8¹/2"x11" paper.) A subtle touch: LeNae glued extra leaf punches overlapping the photos, then drew tendrils among them with a pen, pulling them down into the pumpkin patch. The scarecrow pattern is on page 142.

- **patterned Paper Pizazz™**: grass (by the sheet); barn, burlap, denim (*Country*, also by the sheet); Christmas plaid (*Ho Ho Ho!!!*, also by the sheet)
- **solid Paper Pizazz™**: ivory (*Plain Pastels*); brown, tan (*Solid Muted Colors*); orange, light orange (*Plain Brights*); forest green (*Solid Jewel Tones*)
- **⅞" and ½" wide apple punches**: Marvy® Uchida
- **1" wide balloon, ½" wide maple leaf, ⅝" wide swirl and tear drop punches**: Family Treasures, Inc.
- **brown, black, pink decorative chalks**: Craf-T Products
- **black, brown and green pens**: Zig® Writer
- **page designer**: LeNae Gerig

In the photo, an ancient wisteria against a worn stucco wall makes a background for Chris and Jenny. Amy replicated that background with the stucco paper, cutting brown branches to layer against the wall. The punched leaves get their texture from the ferns paper, and the hanging blossoms were built up from tiny balloon punches cut from a softly patterned purple paper.

- **patterned Paper Pizazz™**: ferns (*Floral Papers*, also by the sheet); purple tiles (*Light Great Background*, also by the sheet); brown handmade (*Handmade Papers*); sand (*Textured Papers*)
- **solid Paper Pizazz™**: ivory (*Plain Pastels*)
- **1¼" long leaf punch**: McGill, Inc.
- **⅜" wide balloon punch**: Marvy® Uchida
- **page designer**: Amy Gustafson

MOVEABLE PARTS

Things that open and close, things that slide, things that dangle—the moving elements on the next six pages are fun to create and just as much fun to play with on the pages!

In a well-known children's story, a wardrobe door opens into a magical new world. Here it's a telephone booth, but a typically British one. The door opens to show scenes of London—certainly a magical new world if you're visiting it for the first time. The vellum lining of the door lets you see just a hint of what's inside. The pattern is on page 142.

- **patterned Paper Pizazz™**: stamps (*Vacation #2*, also by the sheet); cobblestones (*Textured Papers*); vellum with tri-dots (*Vellum Papers*)
- **solid Paper Pizazz™**: red (*Plain Brights*); black (*Solid Jewel Tones*); specialty gold (*Metallic Papers*, also by the sheet)
- **alphabet template**: Frances Meyer, Inc.®
- **black pen**: Marvy® Uchida
- **X-acto® knife and cutting surface**
- **page designer:** Amy Gustafson

Yes, I know you usually push a lawn mower. But just try pulling this one across the page and watch the grass get shorter. (Don't you wish that would work at home?) The background grass strip has a 6"x¼" slit cut in it to ride over the 1/4" squares of foam tape that raise the front grass layer. The mower is mounted on a double thickness of foam to raise it above both grass layers. The pattern is on page 143.

- **patterned Paper Pizazz™**: grass (by the sheet); clouds (*Our Vacation*, also by the sheet)
- **solid Paper Pizazz™**: yellow, blue (*Plain Brights*); black (*Solid Jewel Tones*); specialty gold (*Metallic Papers*, also by the sheet)
- **black and metallic silver pens**: Sakura Gelly Roll
- **X-acto® knife and cutting surface**
- **foam tape**: Scotch® Brand
- **page designer**: Amy Gustafson

A background like this border paper is perfect to highlight a single photo with a fun, easy-to-make pop-up. The outer folder is a 4½"x11" piece folded crosswise. The inner lining was cut slightly smaller, folded backward, then folded forward ¾" away on each side to make the pop-up section (see the side view diagram). The center area was left unglued to lift the photo when the front flap drops down. A tab glued to the back of the 4⅝"x1" top flap slips into a ½" slit cut in the front flap to secure the folder closed. The folded folder and the top flap were matted separately for better separation.

- **patterned Paper Pizazz™**: Sleeping Beauty & fairies, Sleeping Beauty wallpaper (*Disney's Princess Collection*); green with white dots (*Christmas,* also by the sheet)
- **solid Paper Pizazz™**: cream, yellow (*Plain Pastels*)
- **red raffia ribbon**: Plaid Enterprises, Inc.
- **page designer**: Amy Gustafson

photo

¾"

glue here

This three-dimensional Donald Duck jumps up and down in amazement when the tab at the top of the page is pulled. The tab strip extends down behind a ⅛"x1½" slot cut in the background paper. A folded loop extends from the tab through the slot (see the diagram at the left) and Donald is glued to the front of the loop.

The pieced sailor collar at the top of the page draws your attention downward and perfectly echoes Lloyd's (and Donald's) costume.

- **patterned Paper Pizazz™**: blue dots on white, white stars on blue (*Coordinating Colors™ Blue*); white dots on red (*Ho Ho Ho* or by the sheet); Donald, Daisy cut-outs (*Disney's Playtime with Mickey and Friends*)
- **solid Paper Pizazz™**: red, blue, yellow (*Plain Brights*); white (*Plain Pastels*)
- **black pen**: Zig® Writer
- **page designer**: LeNae Gerig

bow pattern

When the wheel is turned, one photo at a time shows through the heart-shaped window. Crop four photos in pie-shaped wedges and mount them on a 6" circle of cardstock to make the wheel. This technique works especially well on a wainscoted page like this one, where the wheel can be concealed behind the upper half of the page with only enough extending to turn the wheel.

- **patterned Paper Pizazz**™: green with stars, blue and white pinstripe (*Dots, Checks, Plaids & Stripes*)
- **solid Paper Pizazz**™: burgundy, dark blue, black (*Solid Jewel Tones*); white (*Plain Pastels*)
- **letter stickers**: Provo Craft®
- **deckle scissors**: Family Treasures, Inc.
- **⅞" wide heart pinch**: McGill, Inc.
- **paper brad**
- **black pen**: Zig® Writer
- **page designer**: Debbie Peterson

Remember how you treasured your first locket? Maybe you put a picture of your Mom or your best friend inside. All day long you kept opening it up to look! You don't have to worry about wearing out the catch on this locket, and you can fit a much larger photo inside! It's made from 3½"-7" long ovals of different sizes—cut the largest from folded paper, with the left side extending ¼ " past the fold to leave a hinge. The chain links are made with two sizes of oval punches and overlapped to drape off the top of the page.

- **patterned Paper Pizazz**™: yellow and gold diamonds, gold crushed suede (*Making Heritage Scrapbook Pages*)
- **solid Paper Pizazz**™: specialty gold (*Metallic Papers*, also by the sheet)
- **colonial scissors**: Fiskars®, Inc.
- **⅜" oval punch**: McGill, Inc.
- **⅝" oval punch**: Family Treasures, Inc.
- **metallic gold pen**: Pentel Gel Roller
- **page designer**: Amy Gustafson

How absolutely fun! A simple pull tab is made from the same patterned paper as the background, so it doesn't need to be concealed. It extends up from Ryan's hat through a 1" slit in the top of the page. Mounting it this way allows the hat to be taken on and off or tipped to either side. A great idea for the hat wearer or bald person in your life!

- **patterned Paper Pizazz™**: purple texture, bright bubbles, red with colored dots (*Bright Great Backgrounds*)
- **solid Paper Pizazz™**: blue, orange (*Plain Brights*)
- **dragonback scissors**: Fiskars®, Inc.
- **black pen**: Zig® Writer
- **page designer**: Amberly Beck

Another pull-tab page contains a jumping dog—it's made like the jumping Donald Duck at the bottom of page 133. LeNae based the colors for her page on the black dog with a red collar in the photo. The combination of two dotted papers gives the page a fun, yet sophisticated look. The pattern for the dog is on page 27.

- **patterned Paper Pizazz™**: black with white dots (by the sheet); red/black checks (by the sheet)
- **solid Paper Pizazz™**: black (*Solid Jewel Tones*); red (*Plain Brights*); white (*Plain Pastels*); brown (*Solid Muted Colors*)
- **1/4" hole punch**: McGill, Inc.
- **small heart punch**: Family Treasures, Inc.
- **puppy die-cut**: Accu/Cut® Systems
- **fat caps alphabet template**: Frances Meyer, Inc.®
- **X-acto® knife and cutting surface**
- **photo mounting tapes**: Fiskars® Inc.
- **black pen**: Zig® Writer
- **white pen**: Pentel Gel Roller
- **page designer**: LeNae Gerig

Ryan spent his time in the park running from one ride to another, so Amberly scrapbooked the photos into a page full of motion. The pinwheel paper quilted background and the spiral punches create movement. The photo of Ryan on the swing is mounted with a brass paper fastener, so it can be swung from side to side. The center top of the photo was left unglued so the fastener doesn't make an ugly lump.

- **patterned Paper Pizazz™**: blue textured, black and colored stripe (*Great Backgrounds*)
- **solid Paper Pizazz™**: red solid (*Plain Brights*); yellow solid (*Plain Pastels*)
- **letter stickers**: Provo Craft®
- ⅝" wide spiral, 1" flower and 1⅜" flower punches: Family Treasures, Inc.
- **mini-scallop scissors**: Fiskars®, Inc.
- **black pen**: Zig® Writer
- **page designer**: Amberly Beck

Like the top of page 134, this page has a wheel which reveals a different photo with each turn. This heel is larger and more complex, although no harder to create. It displays six photos, each cropped in a heart to match the window (the window was matted to make it smaller so it conceals the photo edges). Cut the heart window ¼" from the edge of a 9" dotted circle. Then cut a ⅞"x⅝" window ⅛" below it and a ⅝" circle out of the center. Mat the 9" and ⅝" circles on yellow and black.

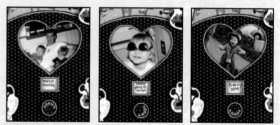

Cut an 8½" red circle and divide into six wedges. Mount a photo and a white journaling plaque in each wedge, laying the dotted circle over them to check the placement. Use a paper fastener through the center to secure the papers to the page. Surround the paper fastener with a double-layered "wall" of ⅛" bits of foam tape, then top it with a ½" circle of foam tape to make a triple thickness. Mount the 9" circle over the red one with ⅛" strips of foam tape—be careful not to get tape on the edges of the red circle, or it won't turn. Write "Turn" on the ⅝" dotted circle and attach it. Attach the page embellishments and journaling on single and double layers of foam tape.

- **patterned Paper Pizazz™**: busy bee (*Annie Lang's Cheerful and Charming*); black with yellow dots (*Bright & Bold*)
- **solid Paper Pizazz™**: yellow, red (*Solid Bright Papers*); black (*Solid Jewel Tones*); white (*Plain Pastels*)
- **Punch-Outs™**: bees (*Annie Lang's Cheerful & Charming*)
- **heart template**: Extra Special Products Corp.
- **black pen**: Sakura Gelly Roll
- **white pen**: Pentel Milky Gel Roller
- **foam mounting tape**: Scotch® Brand
- **paper brad**
- **page designer**: Amy Gustafson

The bottom photo is the moveable part! Silhouette and mat it on white. Tape half a paper clip to the back, so the other end extends below. Cut the top off the oatmeal paper in an irregular wavy line; glue to the bottom of the sky paper. Cut a wavy 3" tall strip of water paper; glue it to the oatmeal paper. Cut a wavy 2" tall strip of light blue, don't glue yet. Use the wave scissors to cut a 1½" tall strip of water paper. Turn it over and glue it to the light blue, then glue to the 3" water strip along the bottom and sides. Slip the paper clip over the top of the light blue wave so you can glide the Wave Runner through the water.

- **patterned Paper Pizazz™**: clouds (*Vacation*, also by the sheet); pool water (*Vacation #2*, also by the sheet)
- **solid Paper Pizazz™**: oatmeal, purple, tan, brown, green, gray (*Solid Muted Colors*); light blue, white, ivory (*Plain Pastels*)
- **brown, black, blue decorating chalk**: Craf-T Products
- **wide wave scissors**: Fiskars®, Inc.
- **1 1/4" paperclip**
- **black pen**: Zig® Writer
- **photo mounting tape**: Scotch® Brand
- **page designer**: LeNae Gerig

A window that opens is one of the simplest moveable devices, and it's always a charming touch—everyone loves a secret! Here the window takes the form of a sideways H cut into a sheet of gingham paper ⅛" smaller than the blue outer mat of the covered photo. The opening edges were trimmed in the same blue, and the journaling plaque was glued only to the left side to make a handle. The whole assembly was glued over the matted photo to reveal it when the window is opened.

- **patterned Paper Pizazz™**: blue plaid, blue windowpane plaid (*Bright Tints*)
- **solid Paper Pizazz™**: dark blue (*Solid Jewel Tones*); white (*Plain Pastels*)
- **black pen**: Zig® Writer
- **page designer**: Susan Cobb

DANGLES

They're fun embellishments that hang from your page in the most interesting ways!

Bow punches along the bottom of the journaling plaque hold dangling matted figures cut from the background paper. Two patterned papers are cut diagonalloy then reglued to make a coordinating 2-page spread. Notice the ribbon glued across the papers. Combining matted and silhouetted photos with raised Punch-Outs™ (attached with foam tape) adds dimension to this page. Like the action in the photos, this is a fun page!

- **patterned Paper Pizazz**™: Easter characters (*Cheerful & Charming*)

- **solid Paper Pizazz**™: green with yellow dots, pink with yellow stitches (*Perfect Pairs*™ *Pink & Blue*); white, green (*Plain Pastels*)
- **bunny Punch-Outs**™: *Cheerful & Charming Punch-Outs*™
- **corner punch:** Family Treasures, Inc.
- **⅞" wide bow punch:** McGill, Inc.
- **cord:** 6" of ⅛" wide silver
- **30" sheer white picot ½"wide ribbon:** Wrights®
- **deckle scissors:** Family Treasures, Inc.
- **page designer:** Debbie Peterson

Chalked clouds and star punches add a dreamy feel to this heavenly design. The cluster of punches overlapping the photo makes it clear who the real star is. More punched stars dangle from lightweight gold thread floating above the page, adding to the airy look.

- **patterned Paper Pizazz**™: moons and clouds (*Annie Lang's Heartwarming Papers*)
- **solid Paper Pizazz**™: yellow (*Solid Muted Colors*); white (*Plain Pastels*)
- **½" star, 1/16" hole punches:** Family Treasures, Inc.
- **blue, pink, white decorating chalk:** Craf-T Products
- **thread:** 12" length of metallic gold
- **black pen:** Zig® Writer
- **page designer:** Shauna Berglund-Immel

The red and black background and accent papers are a beautiful example of picking up colors from the photos. Butterflies and punched hearts reflect the feeling of the occasion, and the silver bow with pretty dangles is a perfect way to tie the couple's names together in a romantic way.

- **patterned Paper Pizazz**™: butterfly stripes (*Perfect Pairs*™ *Red & Black*)
- **solid Paper Pizazz**™: dark red, black (*Solid Jewel Tones*); white (*Plain Pastels*)
- **heart, corner punches**: Family Treasures, Inc.
- **12" of ¹⁄₁₆" silver cord**: Wrights®
- **deckle scissors**: Family Treasures, Inc.
- **white gel pen**: Pentel Milky Gel Roller
- **page designer**: Debbie Peterson

Punched hearts dangling from sparkly iridescent ribbon give a fairy-tale look to this Disneyland Park page. Raising the border with foam tape lets the hearts move freely. Bows cut from an unused border section adorn the computer-journaled plaque and the mats to pull the whole page together.

- **patterned Paper Pizazz**™: Belle border (*Disney's Princess Collection*); roses on speckles, blue speckled (*Lisa Williams Blue, Yellow & Green*)
- **solid Paper Pizazz**™: pink, white (*Plain Pastels*); blue (*Plain Brights*)
- **heart punch**: Marvy® Uchida
- **corner punch**: Memories Forever
- **8" of ¹⁄₃₂" wide iridescent thread**: Wrights®
- **deckle scissors**: Family Treasures, Inc.
- **page designer**: Debbie Peterson

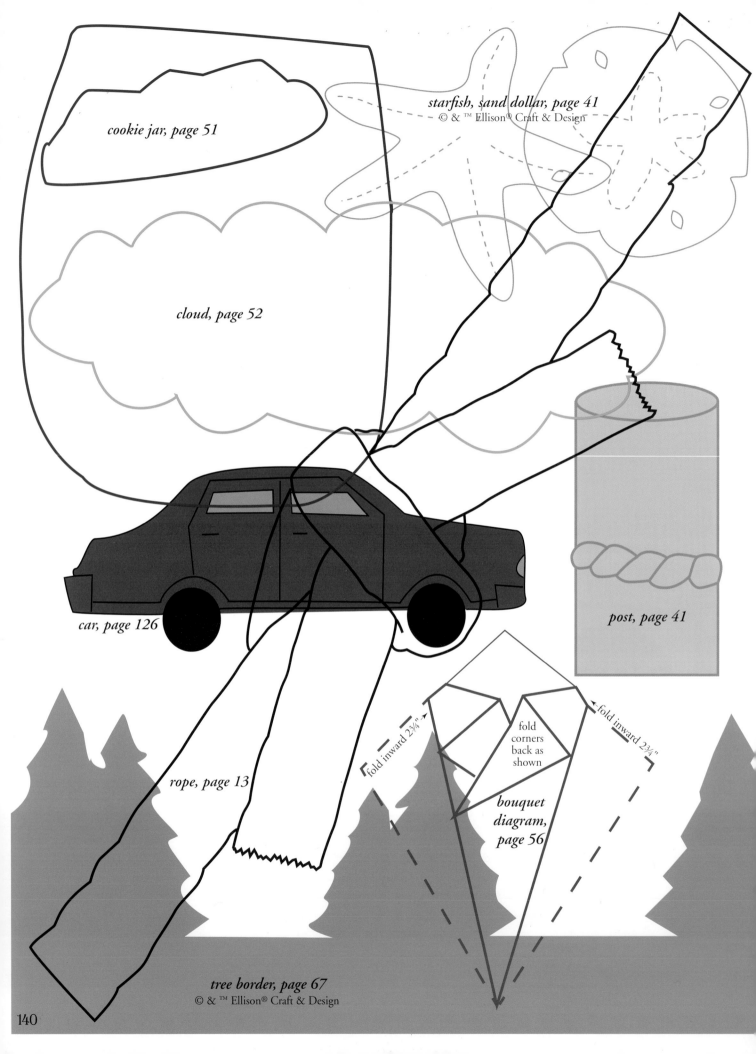

cookie jar, page 51

starfish, sand dollar, page 41
© & ™ Ellison® Craft & Design

cloud, page 52

car, page 126

post, page 41

rope, page 13

fold inward 2¾"

fold corners back as shown

fold inward 2¾"

bouquet diagram, page 56

tree border, page 67
© & ™ Ellison® Craft & Design

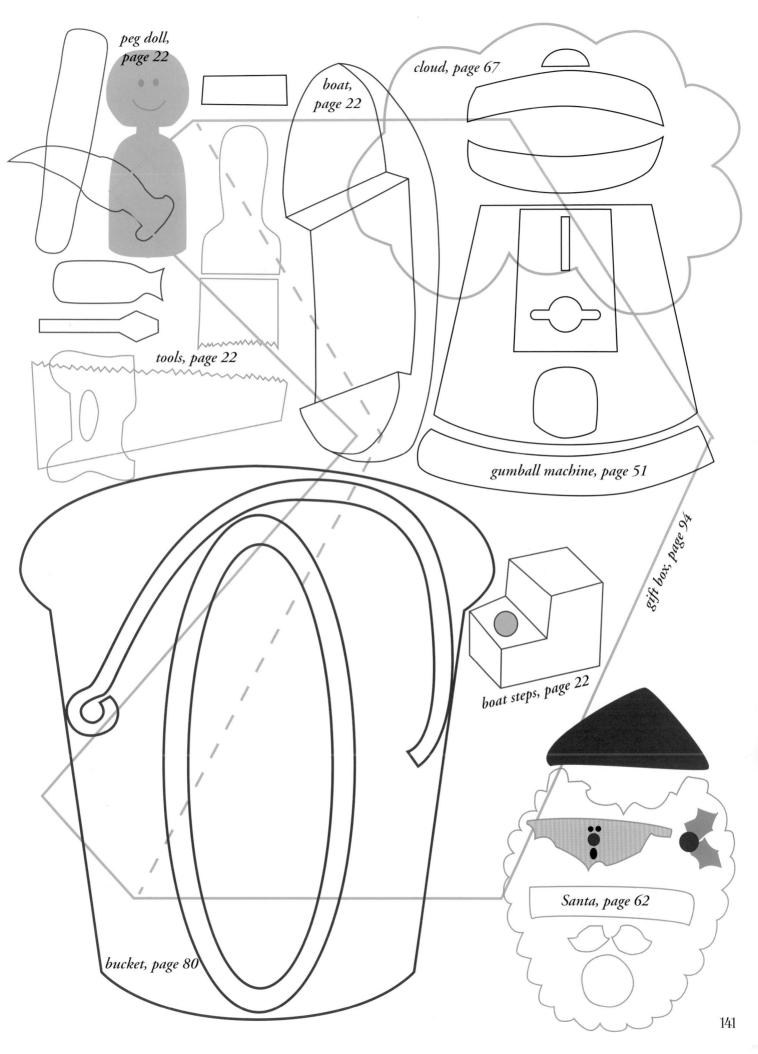

peg doll,
page 22

boat,
page 22

cloud, page 67

tools, page 22

gumball machine, page 51

gift box, page 94

boat steps, page 22

bucket, page 80

Santa, page 62

141

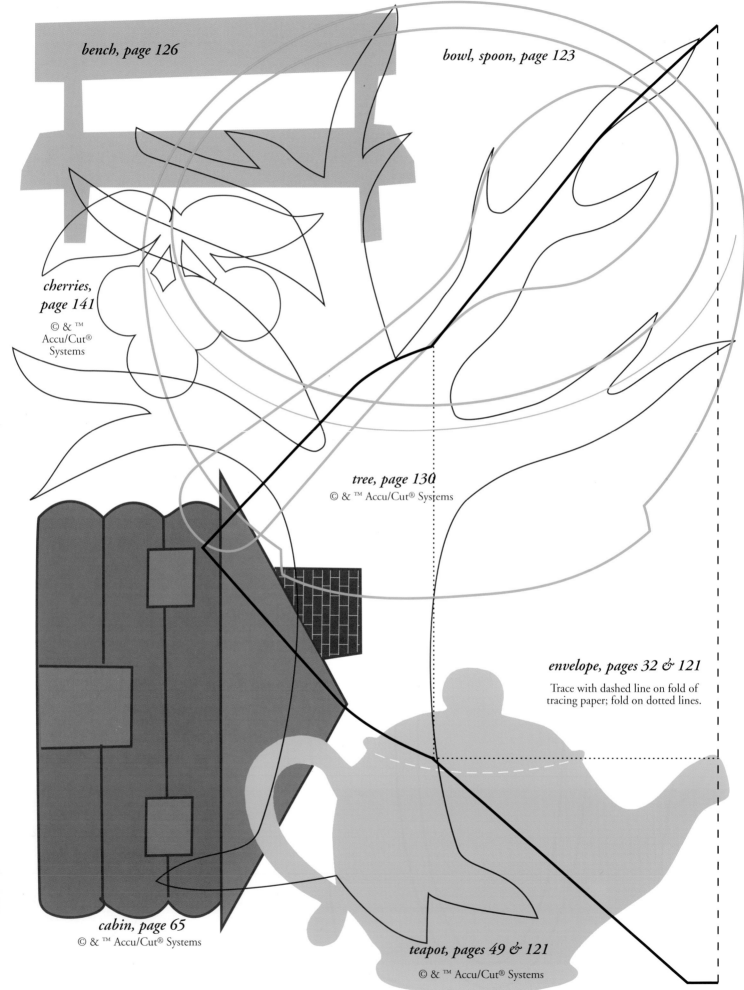

bench, page 126

bowl, spoon, page 123

cherries,
page 141

© & ™
Accu/Cut®
Systems

tree, page 130
© & ™ Accu/Cut® Systems

envelope, pages 32 & 121

Trace with dashed line on fold of
tracing paper; fold on dotted lines.

cabin, page 65
© & ™ Accu/Cut® Systems

teapot, pages 49 & 121

© & ™ Accu/Cut® Systems

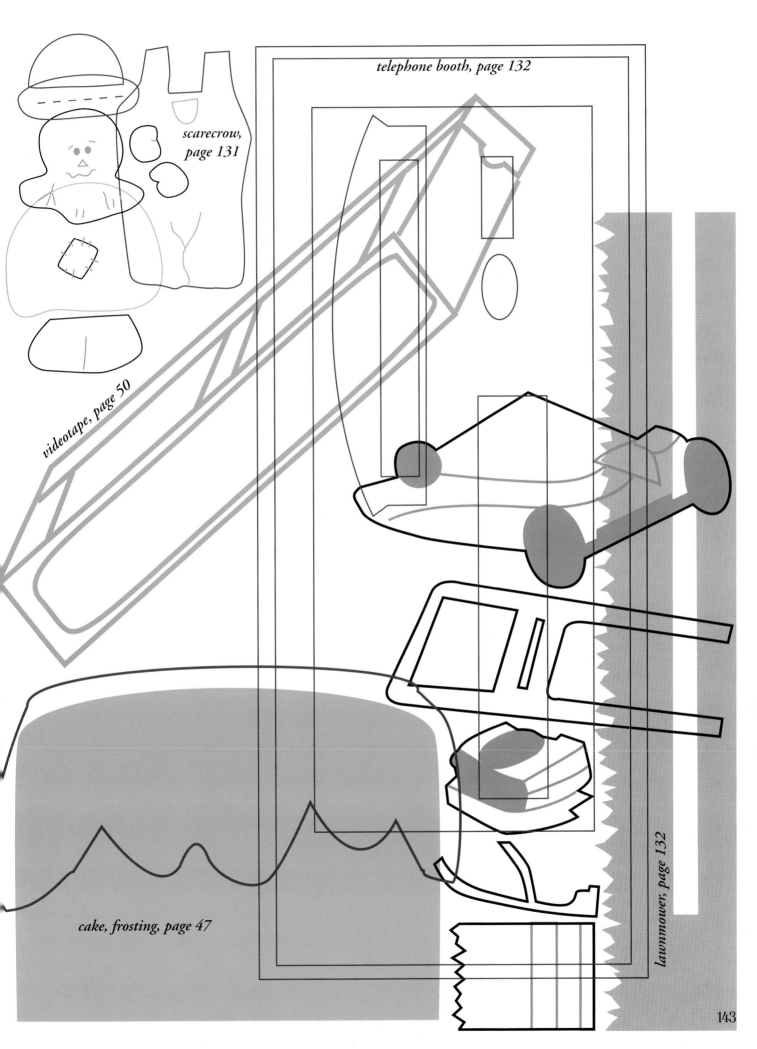

scarecrow, page 131

telephone booth, page 132

videotape, page 50

cake, frosting, page 47

lawnmower, page 132

The Scrapbooker's Bill of Rights

A **Scrapbooker** is entrusted with documenting and safely preserving family photos in an album to be treasured by future generations. Creating a Scrapbook is an honorable and important task. As a Scrapbooker, you are entitled (but not limited) to the following rights:

You have the right to take as long as you want to complete one album page. This may be five minutes or two weeks.

You have the right to purchase a certain scrapbook item for no other reason than because 1) you like it; 2) you think it's cute; 3) you'll never find it again, or; 4) you know you'll use it someday.

You have the right to a workspace of your own. This may be the basement, your college student's old bedroom, or the kitchen table. It's yours.

You have the right to scrapbook when inspiration strikes—whether the dishes are done or not.

You have the right to request peaceful, kid-free, stress-less scrap time—guilt-free.

You have the right to create pages that reflect and celebrate the spirit of the one person who is usually NOT in the photograph: You.

You have the right to put whatever you want on your album page. This includes, but is not limited to: patterned papers, die-cuts, stickers and Punch-Outs™. You may place as many or as few photos per page as you deem appropriate.

You have the right to do nothing more than snack and socialize at a 6-hour cropping party.

You have the right to value your personal scrapbooking style to be as important as your photographs. You are creating a treasure—and part of that treasure is you.

You have the right to create your own legacy, one page at a time.

© 2000 Hot Off The Press, Inc. Canby, OR 97013